POLITICAL THEORY AND IDEOLOGY

MAIN THEMES IN EUROPEAN HISTORY

Bruce Mazlish, General Editor

POLITICAL THEORY AND IDEOLOGY

Edited by
Judith N. Shklar
Harvard University

THE MACMILLAN COMPANY
COLLIER-MACMILLAN LIMITED, LONDON

Third Printing, 1970

Library of Congress catalog card number: 66–10767

The Macmillan Company
Collier-Macmillan Canada, Ltd., Toronto, Ontario

Printed in the United States of America

FOREWORD

History, we are frequently told, is a seamless web. However, by isolating and studying the strands that compose the tapestry of man's past, we are able to discern the pattern, or patterns, of which it is comprised. Such an effort does not preclude a grasp of the warp and woof, and the interplay of the strands; rather, it eventually demands and facilitates such a comprehension. It is with this in mind that the individual volumes of the MAIN THEMES series have been conceived.

The student will discover, for example, that the population changes discussed in one volume relate to the changes in technology traced in another volume; that both changes are affected by, and affect in turn, religious and intellectual developments; and that all of these changes and many more ramify into a complicated historical network through all the volumes. In following through this complex interrelationship of the parts, the student recreates for himself the unity of history.

Each volume achieves its purpose, and its appeal to a general audience, by presenting the best articles by experts in the field of history and allied disciplines. In a number of cases, the articles have been translated into English for the first time. The individual volume editor has linked these contributions into an integrated account of his theme, and supplied a selected bibliography by means of footnotes for the student who wishes to pursue the topic further. The introduction is an original treatment of the problems in the particular field. It provides continuity and background for the articles, points out gaps in the existing literature, offers new interpretations, and suggests further research.

The volumes in this series afford the student of history an unusual opportunity to explore subjects either not treated, or touched upon lightly in a survey text. Some examples are population—the dramatis personae of history; war—the way of waging peace by other means; the rise of technology and science in relation to society; the role of religious and cultural ideas and institutions; the continuous ebb and flow of exploration and colonialism; and the political and economic works contrived by modern man. Holding fast to these Ariadne threads, the student penetrates the fascinating labyrinth of history.

BRUCE MAZLISH
General Editor

CONTENTS

INTRODUCTION

The word "ideology" is so frequently used today that it is easy to forget how very new it is and how uncertain its meaning still remains. Indeed the *Encyclopaedia of the Social Sciences,* a very comprehensive work published as late as 1936, has no entry under that heading. It is no exaggeration to say that until the Second World War, and more especially, the Cold War, very few Americans gave any thought to ideology at all. Even in Europe it was not until the interwar period that ideology became a subject of serious scholarly concern. This situation is not really surprising, since the very term only makes its appearance in the last years of the eighteenth century and has always been bedevilled by controversies about its true significance. From the first, ideology has been used colloquially to refer to any visionary and grandiose scheme of social reform. As such it is a word of opprobrium encompassing all political dreams, whatever their nature. However, the main struggle over the significance of ideology does not involve such common usage.[1] The struggle is, rather, a part of the most serious philosophical disagreements about the structure and meaning of human history. It is, above all, concerned with the place of ideas in the shaping of mankind's social development and, more particularly, the role of political ideas. For whatever else ideology may be, historians now agree that it involves those ideas that seem to form an integral part of political-social history, or at least ideas that are seen in a social context.

The range of disputed issues raised by conflicting philosophies of history has, in the modern age, been enormous. Ideology touches upon

[1] Arne Naess et al., *Democracy, Ideology and Objectivity,* Oslo University Press, Oslo, 1956, offers an account of the conflicting definitions of ideology.

only some of them, but they are of truly central importance. The first question it raises is whether all ideas—political, religious, scientific, or aesthetic—are the direct products of social situations. What do individual thinkers contribute to the history of ideas? Do they express purely personal experiences and reflections, or do they give voice to group minds? What are the significant groups whose situation finds systematic intellectual expression? Are political philosophies a primary part of social history, or merely pale reflections of some other, more "real", set of historical experiences, even though their authors cannot recognize this? Do ideas shape actions and events, or are they just rationalizations of more basic, subrational drives? What sort of unconscious social impulses are at work here? Above all, does history as a whole follow a determinate pattern which allows the historian to identify some social ideas as "progressive", in contrast to "retrogressive" ones, and to regard the former as historically "right", and the latter as "false"? Is the structure of history, moreover, one of successive group struggles, and so, one of rising and declining, victorious and discarded ideas? Some historians reject these notions entirely. They see history as a matter of unique and discrete sets of events and not as a plan or design of any sort, and they avoid historical generalizations as much as possible. The selections in this volume, however, are drawn from authors who, though they disagree on the meaning of ideology, share a belief in the possibility of uncovering schemes of historical development and of finding the true place of political ideas in them. All are meant to illustrate the ways in which theories about history, and so about ideology, have been applied to the interpretation of the history of political ideas. It is hoped that they will reveal both the strengths and the limitations of sociological approaches to political philosophy, without in any way slighting other ways of understanding our intellectual past.

That men's ideas about society are in some measure shaped by their preferences and interests has, of course, always been known. That prejudice and selfishness may distort our perceptions and make us either credulous or willfully untruthful is not a new discovery. Political opponents have never failed to accuse each other of these errors. The core of the eighteenth century's radical attack on traditional religion and politics, for instance, consisted of just such a charge: that clerical superstition and ambition had combined to becloud the minds of generations of Europeans and had been the chief source of all their miseries. It was not, however, then doubted that genuine truth about politics and morality could and would be known to disinterested men of reason. Indeed one of the first tasks of enlightened men was to discover exactly how the human mind worked. Once it was understood where impressions and ideas came from and how they developed, it would become possible through a process of scientific education to remold men in such a way as to render them happy, good, and open to true knowledge. These hopes had been inspired originally by Locke's psychology, and they found their most systematic expression in the work of Destutt de Tracy (1754–1836).[2] In retrospect, it seems ironic that he should have chosen the name *idéologie* for his new science of the mind which was more or less what we would today call the psychology of learning. Because of the radical social implications of this theory, Destutt de Tracy and his fellow *idéologues* eventually were bound to come into conflict with Napoleon. His reconciliation to the Church, no less than the increasingly autocratic character of his regime, were deeply distasteful to these last survivors of the pre-Revolutionary Enlightenment. The Emperor, in turn, despised and harassed not only them, but all those intellectuals whom he indiscriminately called *idéologues* and whom he regarded as uniformly deaf to historical and political realities in their preoccupation with the abstract and universal needs of mankind.[3] In this Napoleon proved to be the wave of the future. That ideology is a form of political moonshine has been the belief of most subsequent "hard-headed" politicians. Like Napoleon they have also suspected these absurd manifestations of being sinister, dangerous, and powerful. Perhaps the intellectual ferment of the century preceding the French Revolution had given Napoleon an especially strong sense of the practical consequences of political speculations. His opponents, particularly the philosophers among them, agreed that public opinion ruled the world and that the men of ideas thus indirectly made history. It was certainly the designers of the many new systems of political philosophy in the nineteenth century who earned it the title, "the age of ideology". Curiously, however, the thinker who contributed most to the entire history of ideology, Karl Marx, did not regard philosophers or their works as actors of primary importance on

[2] For a general history of the idea of ideology up to Nietzsche see Hans Barth, *Wahrheit und Ideologie*, Eugen Rentsch Verlag, Zürich, 1961.

[3] Jay W. Stern, *The Mind and the Sword*, Twayne Publishers, New York, 1961.

the stage of history. That is why, among other things, he was the founder of the modern theory of ideology.

Marx's contribution to the theory of ideology lies, above all, in his philosophy of history. The history of the past, according to Marx, is the history of class struggles.[4] Classes are defined in terms of their position in the productive process and of their social power. The latter depends upon the degree of control they exercise over the means of production. From time to time, moreover, the economic and technological creations of man render existing social relations obsolete, as a new, more powerful, and competent class becomes aware of its potentialities and challenges the domination exercised by an older class. If the latter has really lost the material basis for its position, then a successful revolution will occur, such as the French Revolution of 1789 in which the bourgeoisie overthrew an exhausted feudal aristocracy. At all times, however, not just in revolutionary periods, society is torn by class hostilities which give each epoch its specific character. This state of affairs will prevail until the last proletarian revolution abolishes all classes.

In the course of these struggles it is the material "substructure" of society, the daily struggle for subsistence and the direct experiences of men in their economic relationships, which is fundamental in forming the spirit of an age. To be quite exact, one should say the various spirits of an age, since the warring classes do not share in a common outlook. Far from it. For the proletariat, for instance, "law, morality, religion . . . are so many bourgeois prejudices, behind which lurk in ambush just as many bourgeois interests".[5] Furthermore, ideas in general—for any class—constitute a "superstructure", expressing and ordering the more basic human experiences.[6] They are, as such, only reflections of an "objective" historical situation, rather than part of its essential structure. In the constant process of change through struggle they play a secondary role. To be sure, until a class reaches full consciousness of its destiny, until it becomes aware of its collective character and "objective" social situation, it cannot act, but it will reach this stage of mental development in any case, once the material conditions are ripe. And no amount of social awareness or outraged moral sense

[4] Karl Marx and Friedrich Engels, *Manifesto of the Communist Party,* in Lewis S. Feuer, *Marx and Engels: Basic Writings on Politics and Philosophy,* Doubleday & Co., New York, 1959, p. 7.

[5] *Ibid.,* p. 18.

[6] *A Contribution to the Critique of Political Economy,* in Feuer, *op. cit.,* pp. 43–44.

will be of any avail if the prevailing economic structure of the time is not ready for revolutionary political action. That is why pre-Marxian socialists were, for all their good intentions, historical failures. The refusal to recognize this, the real relationship between material existence and ideas, was precisely what Marx called ideology. In ideology "men and their circumstances appear upside down, as in a *camera obscura*".[7] Law, morality, and metaphysics all share this distorted vision and all are, therefore, false, deceptive means of sustaining the present social order.

Since the mature Marx's main interests were economics and political action, he did not devote more than passing notice to the history of political theory. He never, for example, showed in any detail how the substructure of any given period had determined specific philosophies. In his younger years, however, he had undertaken an intense critique of religion, a subject to which he occasionally returned. It is this part of his writings that is the clearest forerunner of most future theories of ideology. Religion, Marx believed, arose when the division of labor began to alienate man from the work of his hands. In religion men found both a consolation for their actual sufferings, and a vision of an existence which was the exact opposite of their actual situation. As such, religion was both a means of escape from daily suffering and the vehicle for rebellious feelings of the socially helpless and hopelessly weak.[8] When the material conditions creating their misery would disappear, dreams would be replaced by action and religion, the mirror and instrument of oppression, would vanish forever. In the meantime, since it is the duty of philosophers to alter the world, religion must be exposed for the sham it is so that men might be liberated from it. This method of political warfare, by which ideas are "unmasked" to reveal their "real" social roots, was to become the standard technique of ideological warfare in the decades that followed. Marx and Engels employed this weapon in their attacks upon all rival socialists, whose ideas they tried to destroy, not by showing them to be untrue or illogical, but by "exposing" their hidden class character and tendency to serve the existing state of society.[9] Eventually, to be sure, all political parties came to practice this form of "psychic annihilation" in their

[7] Karl Marx and Friedrich Engels, *The German Ideology,* in Feuer, *op. cit.,* p. 247.

[8] Karl Marx, *Toward a Critique of Hegel's Philosophy of Right,* in Feuer, *op. cit.,* pp. 262–263.

[9] Karl Marx, *The Class Struggle in France,* in Feuer, *op. cit.,* pp. 316–317.

mutual struggles, but as Karl Mannheim has said, "socialism in its analysis of ideology worked out a coherent, critical method which was, in effect, an attempt to annihilate the antagonists' utopia by showing that they had their roots in the existing situation".[10] The ferreting out of the social determinants—and so the bias—of the thinking of all his opponents did not for a moment lead Marx to question the roots of his own thinking, which he regarded as scientifically true and in no sense ideological. Marx was no relativist. He clearly believed in the absolute truth of the positive sciences and counted his economics among them. In the classless society, moreover, all the obstacles to the pursuit of truth would necessarily be greatly reduced. Ideology was thus only a specific form of untruth, created by the class system, and one that would disappear as it was unmasked.

In the decades immediately following Marx's death, his followers became increasingly uneasy about the materialist theory of the "superstructure." Among academic socialists the history of ideas was investigated to discover precursors and paradigmatic figures, who were somehow socialists before the time was right, but whose moral insight created a socialist tradition. It was this tradition which permitted the intellectual integration of socialism into the European intellectual past. This, rather than the material substructure and class situations to which these ideas corresponded, now became the main object of socialist historical study.[11] Socialism was clearly becoming respectable. A late letter from Engels, written in 1893 to his fellow socialist Mehring, already clearly provided the rationale for this shift in emphasis.

One more point is lacking, which however, Marx and I always failed to stress enough. That is to say, we all laid, and *were bound* to lay, the main emphasis, in the first place, on the *derivation* of political, juridical, and other ideological notions, and of actions arising through the medium of these notions, from basic economic facts. But in so doing we neglected the formal side—the ways and means by which these notions, etc., come about—for the sake of the content.

Ideology is a process accomplished by the so-called thinker consciously, it is true, but with a false consciousness. The real motive forces impelling him remain unknown to him; otherwise it simply would not be an ideologi-

[10] Karl Mannheim, *Ideology and Utopia,* Harvest Books, Harcourt, Brace and Co., New York, n.d. pp. 38–41, p. 241.

[11] E.g., Eduard Bernstein, *Cromwell and Communism,* translated by H. J. Stenning, Allen and Unwin, London, 1930; Karl Kautsky, *Thomas More and his Utopia,* translated by H. J. Stenning, Russell, New York, 1959.

cal process. Hence he imagines false or seeming motive forces. Because it is a process of thought, he derives its form as well as its content from pure thought, either his own or that of his predecessors. He works with mere thought material, which he accepts without examination as the product of thought, and does not investigate further for a more remote source independent of thought; indeed, this is a matter of course to him, because as all action is mediated by thought it appears to him to be ultimately based upon thought.

The historical ideologist (historical is here simply meant to comprise the political, juridical, philosophical, theological—in short, all the spheres belonging to society and not only to nature) thus possesses in every sphere of science material which has formed itself independently out of the thought of previous generations and has gone through its own independent course of development in the brains of these successive generations. True, external facts belonging to one or another sphere may have exercised a co-determining influence on this development, but the tacit presupposition is that these facts themselves are also only the fruits of a process of thought, and so we still remain within that realm of mere thought, which apparently has successfully digested even the hardest facts. . . .

Hanging together with this is the fatuous notion of the ideologists that because we deny an independent historical development to the various ideological spheres which play a part in history we also deny them any effect upon history. The basis of this is the common undialectical conception of cause and effect as rigidly opposite poles, the total disregarding of interaction. These gentlemen often almost deliberately forget that once a historic element has been brought into the world by other, ultimately economic causes it reacts, can react on its environment and even on the causes that have given rise to it. . . .

In fact, in the years preceding the First World War the tendency to "reduce" philosophy to something more "real", but less rational, was more characteristic of the enemies of socialism than of the socialists. The emphasis on the irrational character of individual and social development appeared to be particularly compatible with traditionalist and authoritarian political attitudes. It was, thus, Nietzsche and Pareto, the declared enemies of all humanitarian and democratic movements, who were most given to "uncovering" the instinctual and even predatory motives beneath all political beliefs and actions. For them it was, to be sure, not class affiliation or the economic structure of society that determined thought. Quite in keeping with their generally individualistic outlooks they looked to psychology to reveal the limitations of rationality, and so, the most deep-seated obstacles to any possible social reform.

The reformers themselves were, after all, only expressing irrational personal power drives. Nietzsche even used these psychological notions to build a theory of history clearly designed to refute both Marxism and the liberal faith in painless progress. In his view there were only two moralities, corresponding to two basic human types that recur regularly throughout history. According to Nietzsche all social and religious thought expresses the aspirations of either the slaves or the masters.[12] Each one of these types has its own will to power. Since classical antiquity, however, the magnanimous heroic man has suffered nothing but defeat at the hands of resentful slave-man. From Christianity onward every social movement, of which democracy is but the latest version, has expressed the psychic needs and ambitions of the slaves.[13] The entire history of philosophy in the West, with its asceticism, is but an assertion of the philosophers' will to power, itself a manifestation of antiheroic drives.[14] This division of mankind into two primary antagonistic psychological types—like Pareto's insistence that all theories can be reduced to a few widely shared subrational "residues", or direct preferences which "really" determine conduct, whatever theory "rationalizes" them—is too general to be applied to the analysis of any specific system of thought.[15] Moreover, it does scant justice to the actual complexities of both individual and social typology. As an instrument of criticism of an increasingly collectivist age, it was, nevertheless, highly effective. Furthermore, psychology has, in fact, come to reveal the hold of nonrational drives upon human thought, expression, and conduct. However, for many years it did not contribute much to the theory of ideology or to the study of social history because it was preeminently concerned with individual irrationalities and not with collective, socially shared ones.

Although there was plenty of ideological conflict in the years preceding the First World War, it was the Russian Revolution which gave a new impetus to revolutionary Marxist thinking. Revolutionary situations and ideas attracted the attention of historians with particular

[12] Friedrich Nietzsche, *Beyond Good and Evil,* in *The Philosophy of Nietzsche,* Modern Library, Random House, New York, n.d., pp. 578–580.

[13] *Ibid.*, p. 494.

[14] *Ibid.*, pp. 386–387 and *The Geneology of Morals, Ibid.*, pp. 729–730, 745–747.

[15] E.g., Vilfredo Pareto, *The Mind and Society* translated by Andrew Bongiorno and Arthur Livingston, Harcourt, Brace & Co., New York, 1935, Vol. III s. 1416.

intensity. Marxist scholars, especially, came to seek eagerly for evidence of revolutionary conflicts and ideas in the past. This search for precursors of the Russian Revolution made the English Civil War and the French Revolution favorite subjects of research for those who lived in the expectation of imminent revolution. For them the rise of the bourgeoisie and its struggle with the feudal order fulfilled a vital exemplary role that needed the closest scrutiny if similar events in the present were to be fully understood. In the present volume there are three selections to illustrate the contemporary Marxist approach to the history of political theory. The first, Christopher Hill's essay on Hobbes, depicts the latter as a typically bourgeois thinker. However, after pointing to Hobbes' middle-class origins, it does not dwell on that point, but merely describes how novel and prophetic of an entirely new era Hobbes' ideas were. It is an account with which few scholars would argue, though they might offer other explanations for Hobbes' undeniable modernity than his birth and immediate surroundings. The "objective" basis of political theory receives far more emphasis in C. B. Macpherson's study of Locke. Here clearly as much is to be inferred about the historic state of the "bourgeois" England of Locke's day as about Locke's thought. The latter, moreover, is seen as covering a multitude of tacit assumptions. As such it is revealed as a piece of essentially bourgeois ideology, which offered little in the way of either equality or liberty to the majority of Englishmen. The contradictions in Locke are taken as signs of class preferences and affiliations which, though they did not fit the moral promise of liberalism, corresponded only too closely to the actualities of social life in the age of bourgeois ascendency. Thus Locke's ideas were above all an expression of the "objectively" bourgeois character of his age, and his greatness lies precisely in having expressed so well the ideology of the class that had just come into its own historically and that was destined to dominate the new age. Lastly, Harold Laski's account of the ideas of Voltaire and the French Enlightenment again points to their "bourgeois" character by showing the contempt in which the poor were held. Since the French Revolution had long been regarded as *the* bourgeois revolution par excellence, this, the objective circumstance, is less stressed than Voltaire's actual utterances, but these are nevertheless meant, above all, to illustrate the main historical assumption: that it was a middle-class age whose aspirations and interests were hostile to those of the vast majority of propertyless men.

In many ways the Marxism here displayed is of a relatively crude and undialectical nature. Ideology is identified as an expression of direct economic class interest, and ideas are seen as the simple and immediate effects of social circumstances. The notion of classes is also a rather simple one, reduced, essentially, to the "haves" and the "have-nots." There is also an element of moral outrage at a conspiracy to deceive and defraud, that is clearly evident in Macpherson's and Laski's strictures upon their respective bourgeois ideologists. In all this these writings are quite representative of the vulgarization of Marxism that became prevalent everywhere in the years since the First World War.

Although conventional Marxist writings on the history of ideology have been neither very original nor illuminating, Marx, nevertheless, did inspire the most daring and influential of all contemporary theories of ideology, Karl Mannheim's "sociology of knowledge". It is, moreover, a debt that is freely acknowledged.[16] Like Marxism, Mannheim's sociology is a speculative philosophy of history. Although he rejected the Marxian picture of a struggle between three essentially economic classes with a predictable ending, he too saw history as a pattern of struggles between well-defined groups. If these groups were seen in political, geographic, and occupational terms also, they remained primarily economic classes, even though they were more numerous than the classical three. Also, like many of his contemporaries, Mannheim was not a dialectical thinker. He thought that ideas were immediate emanations of social interests, without recognizing, as Engels had noticed, that ideas in their turn structure experience and that there is an interplay between various levels of social experience rather than a simple line of cause and effect from the "real" substructure to the ephemeral superstructure. Lastly, like many non-Marxian philosophers, Mannheim believed that history was a succession of identifiable epochs, each one of which constituted a real entity, a whole, all of whose parts fitted into a pattern. Each one of these eras has its assigned term, so that from its rise to its fall the historian could retrospectively retrace its predetermined path. Not surprisingly, Mannheim felt nothing but contempt for those historians who do not seek general laws and patterns in history, but are content simply to trace the succession of related, but unique, men and events. He thought this approach "naive" because it neither sought nor found the hidden and "real" forces in history. To be sure, he admitted that once one expected to "uncover" secret driving

[16] Karl Mannheim, *Ideology and Utopia,* Routledge and Kegan Paul Ltd., London, 1936, p. 277.

forces beneath the surface of historical life, one found just what one had assumed all along one would find.[17] He was, however, convinced that these assumptions were true and necessary if historical knowledge was to help one to understand man and society. Particularly,

> The study of intellectual history can and must be pursued in a manner which will see in the sequence and co-existence of phenomena more than mere accidental relationships, and will seek to discover in the totality of the historical complex the role, significance and meaning of each component element.[18]

Above all, the history of ideas will become a new "technique for diagnosing the culture of an epoch" by showing everywhere "the interrelationships between the intellectual point of view held and the social position occupied".[19]

Since Mannheim's main interest was the history of political ideas, it was to this study that the sociology of knowledge was first applied, rather than to any other possible field of knowledge. However, he undoubtedly believed that all forms of thought were equally rooted in group life, and that all could be explained only in sociological terms. For "strictly speaking it is incorrect to say that the single individual thinks. Rather . . . he participates in thinking further what other men thought before him".[20] Biography, the individual's personal life-history, is thus insufficient for explaining his ideas, nor will any purely formal analysis of these do. Only the uncovering of the irrational and collective forces that "really" determine political ideas can bring us to a full understanding of them. Mannheim was hopeful that presently all the influences that structure class-judgments and their relations to class-interests would be revealed.[21] Then, at last, a fully self-conscious, self-critical, and so, fully objective, group of historians would exist: the first men to be able to view and to direct society in a truly scientific way.[22] As such, the new sociology of knowledge would amount to a complete break with the entire past history of ideas. It was to be the last revolution. For in the past, according to Mannheim, there had been only two sorts of political ideas: ideologies and utopias. Ideologies, in

[17] *Ibid.*, pp. 175, 201.
[18] *Ibid.*, p. 93.
[19] *Ibid.*, p. 78.
[20] *Ibid.*, p. 3.
[21] *Ibid.*, pp. 162–163.
[22] *Ibid.*, pp. 49–50.

his view, were the typical thought orientation of established or dominant classes, which were inevitably deceived or deceiving in their refusal to recognize the demands of the future. Theirs is consequently always a "false consciousness", a set of interests and values that have no future, no chance of historical realization.[23] Utopias, on the other hand, are the theories of those aspiring classes that are the bearers of an historical destiny and which in time will succeed in forming the effective nucleus of a culture.[24] To be sure, not even successful ideas are capable of driving men to action. Ideas are but a passive element in history. The individual merely gives voice to vital "collective impulses" and the groups themselves are animated not by ideas but by elemental "ecstatic organic" impulses, and by immediate social interests.[25] In sum, then, Mannheim's study of ideas was designed to "reduce" systems of ideas to something that he regarded as more real. Moreover, in the drama of history, they occupied a very modest place. The star actors were impersonal material forces and irrational groups which played out their predetermined struggles, as one after the other rises, declines, and falls before the eyes of the philosophic historian.

Three selections in this volume are designed to illustrate the way in which the sociology of knowledge has been used to interpret the history of political ideas. Alfred von Martin's study of the Renaissance is based on the belief that the rise and fall of the bourgeoisie does not form, as Marx had thought, a single epoch in history, but is, rather, a recurrent phenomenon. The Italian Renaissance is thus seen as a "whole", a complete unit whose entire life can be traced by following the ascent, victory, and decline of the bourgeoisie of that epoch. Their utopia in its progressive, upward movement inspired humanism, the aesthetic flowering, and, indeed, the entire culture of that brilliant era. Their ideologist, in their days of decline, was Machiavelli. The so-called first modern political thinker was, really, the last voice of a decaying class and a dying age. Like other future spokesmen of a frightened and embittered bourgeoisie he was a quintessential fascist, the champion of despotism, a destructive genius, who understood, as he deplored, the decadence around him, but could offer only an unreal, unhistoric ideology built on myths of Roman virtue and might.

There are also here two pieces by Mannheim himself on the

[23] *Ibid.*, pp. 194–196.
[24] *Ibid.*, pp. 205–223.
[25] *Ibid.*, pp. 207, 213–224.

"utopian" reactions to liberalism: first the conservative and then the Marxian. Both were, in Mannheim's terms, genuine utopias, since both can be retrospectively recognized as political visions with a significant historical future, both expressing the aspirations of classes that, in very different ways, were to play a central role in their respective epochs. Both eventually, became, as they were bound to, mere ideologies. In time they and the groups whose experiences they expressed played out their assigned roles and ceased to have a creative future function. The conservative critique of liberalism, as well as its discovery of history as an organic growth, represented especially the reaction of the remaining feudal and rural elements in Germany. For a brief period in the nineteenth century they and their views inspired and dominated the cultural scene. Presently, however, socialism overcame both the liberal and conservative past. Borrowing a sense of history from conservatism, and a ruthlessly forward-looking activism from liberalism, Marx was the heir of both, to become in his turn the central force of an age. This age, Mannheim thought, was now past and done with, as the classless society was at hand, and Marxism, the last of all possible utopias was now just an ideology, even though Marx had not been able to foresee that this would be the fate of his doctrine also.

The most serious deficiency of Mannheim's sociology of knowledge was its failure to concern itself with the psychological mechanisms by which social conditions are translated by groups and individuals into doctrines. Without any account of just how the "objective" world, the structure of society, eventually is reflected in philosophy, in art and in science, the sociology of knowledge must remain an hypothesis, as yet unproven.[26] Eventually it was from among the unorthodox, indeed dissident, followers of Freud that an effort to supply the theory of ideology with a psychology was made. In America few writers on this subject have been more influential than Erich Fromm, especially through his widely read book *Escape from Freedom*. It pictures, among other things, a search for some middle point between the individualism of psychoanalysis and the collectivist sociology of Marx and his various heirs. Unlike Freud, he sees the problem of psychology as that of "the specific kind of relatedness of the individual to the world, and not as

[26] It appears that Mannheim became aware of this deficiency and was increasingly interested in Freudian psychology in his last years. Karl Mannheim, *Essays on Sociology and Social Psychology*, ed. by Paul Kecskemeti, Routledge and Kegan Paul Ltd. London, 1953, pp. 3–6, 267–278.

that of the satisfaction or frustration of this or that instinctual need *per se*." [27] However, he does not go as far as Mannheim in rejecting the value of the genetic or biographical method of analyzing individual men and their thoughts. To understand the great creators of belief-systems and philosophies requires first of all an understanding of their personalities.[28] Social character, for Fromm, does not comprise the whole of an individual's personality, but only those traits he shares with his contemporaries as a result of shared experiences.[29] Social psychology, therefore, concerns itself primarily, not with tracing the social origins of individual thinkers, but with the process by which some ideas, in every age, receive widespread acceptance among large numbers of people. Ideology, here, refers not to all ideas, but just to those that seem to meet some general psychic need in any given age, as Protestantism did in the sixteenth century and fascism did in the twentieth century, for instance.[30] Fromm's theory of history remained completely Marxian, to be sure. The Age of the Reformation is "objectively" that of emerging capitalism, while fascism is the ideological outcome of monopoly capitalism. The economic system creates the "objective" situation that determines all the modes of experience for the individual.[31] What is novel in Fromm's theory is the concern for the *ways* in which external, general situations impinge upon the character structure of individuals. Though there is no fixed human nature, he argues that men are not infinitely malleable and that psychic forces have a dynamism of their own and follow their own laws of development in response to the historical circumstances which act upon them.[32] Instead of focussing solely on such obvious motives as class interest and economic aspirations, for example, one must necessarily turn to such psychic manifestations as anxiety, insecurity and their opposites or, to understand why men come to embrace this or that doctrine. For ideas only become powerful social forces—real ideologies—when they do correspond to a widely felt psychic need. The study of ideology is, therefore, to be the study of the interactions between the permanent psychological needs of men and the

[27] Erich Fromm, *Escape from Freedom,* Rinehart and Co., New York, 1941, p. 12.
[28] *Ibid.,* pp. 64–65.
[29] *Ibid.,* p. 277.
[30] *Ibid.,* p. 22.
[31] *Ibid.,* p. 18.
[32] *Ibid.,* pp. 14–15, 22–23, 279.

changing structure of the historical world into which they are born.[33]

Michael Walzer's study of Puritanism as an ideology, partly reprinted here, is an attempt to take up Fromm's challenging suggestions and to apply them to a concrete case. The primary emphasis here is no longer on either the "objective" historical situation (early capitalism), or on the group character of thinking, both of which are taken for granted. The object of Walzer's scrutiny is a group of *minds* and the way that quite specific shared personal experiences led a group of men to interpret and judge their world. This group's mind is, moreover, in no sense a passive receptacle into which "objective" conditions simply put ideas. Men do not simply respond to an imprint somehow made upon them, but are seen to restructure a situation by internalizing experience and then acting upon a reality which is not just "out there". Ideology here is seen as an interaction of many levels of experience which finds expression in both thought and behavior. If this view makes for a less simple cause-and-effect sequence, it surely does come closer to the rich texture of actual historical life.

Another way of reconstructing a picture of a group mind is illustrated by Louis Hartz's essay on a much larger body of men than the Puritans, the sum of politically articulate Americans at the time of the Revolution. The "objective" state of America, according to Hartz, is a paradoxical one, in that although there were and are economic classes, the one class that had the deepest impact upon the European mind never existed here: the feudal aristocracy. The socio-psychological consequences of the *absence* of this class, and of the struggles against it, have shaped all American political thought and created a uniquely American ideology, just as much as its *presence* has given Europe its own peculiar character. The American bourgeoisie, because it never faced a feudal aristocracy, failed to develop that mixture of resentment of and admiration for aristocratic values and also any sense of identity as a class apart from others. The result is an "irrational Lockeanism", a belief that there is only one set of values because there is only one class, the bourgeoisie, which is not even aware of itself as a class. Taking itself to be a universal order, such a bourgeoisie puts forward libertarian and egalitarian ideology as the only possible one, even when its ideologists are pursuing ends which are in no sense liberal or demo-

[33] *Ibid.*, p. 281.

cratic. It also creates a public mind hostile to and unfamiliar with ideological obstacles and new values which might challenge the self-evidently true ethos. Conflict is regarded as eccentric, agreement as natural, and those remnants of aristocratic society, individuality, differentiation of tastes and manners, and self-assertiveness are discouraged in a social character that seeks security in conformity and unity in alikeness. It gives rise to political ideas which are alike in that they reflect a middle-class mind whose ascendency has never even been in doubt. If this analysis owes much to the Marxian theory that history must be the story of class struggles, it is also a significant departure from it, in recognizing the immense, independent power of psychological forces and their consequences, even if these can ultimately be traced back to a single source in the class structure of a society. Moreover, the recognition that the lack of one or another class may account for the cultural differences between societies is itself an addition to the study of comparative cultures and ideologies.

The new psychological study of political ideas and ideology is clearly not compatible with an extreme materialism or any simple class theory of history. It is thus quite far removed from Marx and even from Mannheim. There is, however, one aspect of the latter's sociology of knowledge that has coincided with the views of many social theorists who did not share his general outlook. This is the theory of the role of the intellectuals in the modern world. The "free intelligentsia", according to Mannheim, lacking both ecclesiastical control and class ties, was *the* most important factor in modern intellectual life.[34] This relatively class-less stratum has given the modern mind its "dynamic and elastic" quality. Its members have been able to ally themselves with any class they chose and to supply it with an ideology. It was they who forced ideas into the political arena.[35] In a hopeful vein, Mannheim foresaw a great mission for this free intelligentsia. As a class-less group they alone were in a position, potentially at least, to become perfectly objective in their social outlook, and thus liberated from ideology and irrationality would lead a new scientifically planned democratic society.[36] Without in the least accepting this vision of the future glories of this intellectual élite, many conservative and liberal writers agreed

[34] *Ideology and Utopia*, pp. 10–13.

[35] *Ibid.*, pp. 153–164.

[36] Karl Mannheim, *Freedom, Power and Democratic Planning*, Routledge and Kegan Paul Ltd., London, 1950.

that the intelligentsia as a rootless group had indeed dominated the capitalist era and had contrived to undermine and ultimately to destroy it. Although they were the inevitable by-products of the capitalist order, they were bound to become its worst enemies. Joseph A. Schumpeter's reflections on the contribution of the intellectuals to the decline of capitalism, here reprinted, perfectly represent this point of view. It is one that has deep roots in both the liberalism and the conservatism of the last century, which ascribed an enormous power for either good or evil to the men who shaped public opinion. In Schumpeter's view all anti-capitalist ideologies express the experiences and interests of these intellectuals, even when they have been foisted upon other classes, especially the workers.

Schumpeter's view of ideology is a sociological one, based still on a class analysis of history, although he was inclined to pay more attention to noneconomic factors, such as military organization and power, in structuring society. There have, however, always been thinkers, especially among theologians, who see ideas and beliefs as disembodied forces exercising a dominant influence upon the lives of individuals and groups. It is not extravagant to call this an "intellectual determinism."[37] All history is seen as a combat between beliefs, true and false, the modern age, however, being viewed especially as one of heresy. The events of our time, as indeed of any period in history, are considered mere reflections of religious beliefs or un-beliefs, and modern ideologies are, above all, heresies from which have sprung innumerable social evils. For they dominate us, as Christianity dominated the Europe of the Middle Ages. From Luther to the "apocalyptic" views of Marx, the origins of totalitarian ideologies have been traced in the minutest detail to show the significance and overwhelming power of heresy in history.

It has indeed been among observers of the governments of Nazi Germany and the Soviet Union that there has been the greatest tendency to stress the role of ideology in shaping political life. This is scarcely surprising, since most Americans only became aware of ideology when they were confronted with these new and hostile political systems. The resulting overspiritualization has received a moderate, but firm, refutation in the selection on totalitarian ideology by Carl J. Friedrich and Zbigniew K. Brzezinski. While accepting the notion that totalitarian ideologies are "secular religions", the authors feel that it is

[37] Judith N. Shklar, *After Utopia*, Princeton University Press, Princeton, 1957, pp. 185–217.

impossible to treat the history of the Soviet Union and of Nazi Germany as the simple working out of Marxism and racism respectively. Moreover, the emphasis ought to be put less on the content of these ideologies than on their symbolic and psychological functions within the totalitarian order as a whole. The only really important element in their teachings, the one that sets them apart from all other ideologies, is the glorification of violence. Their mass appeal may well be in just that. In sum, while totalitarian ideologies may draw upon many traditions of political thinking, it is their current use as instruments of mass organization and violent political warfare that is crucial to our understanding of their place in the contemporary world, and not their nonexistent intellectual force. They can be studied only as an integral aspect, but only one among many others, of an operative totalitarian political system, not as an independent historical or spiritual phenomenon.

Totalitarian ideologies, especially when seen in this light, raise anew the whole question of the relations of ideology to political theory —and in the sharpest of terms. First of all, the various views of ideology that derive from Marx presuppose a considerable degree of freedom. It is simply assumed that ideas can and do emanate spontaneously from material life and find an open expression. The conditions that prevail in contemporary repressive societies, however, with their immense power of controlling every facet of mental life, simply do not allow this process to occur. The end of ideology begins first of all in totalitarian societies.[38] Second, the "reductionism" of the recent past, which was so concerned to "uncover" the common social sources of all thinking and the deceptive function of ideas, has obviously nothing to say about the vast qualitative difference between the sloganlike utterances that act as cohesives for mass parties and the reflections of the great political theorists of the past and the work of the best contemporary social scientists. It has nothing to say about the very evident differences in the function, effect and character of such totally different forms of thinking. In short, it neither can provide, nor was meant to provide, standards for qualitative discrimination. That is, however, what comparative history demands now. It may well be that the social atmosphere which once rendered the sociology of knowledge, for instance, so relevant and persuasive, has now changed. The widely

[38] For a contrary view see Herbert Marcuse, *Soviet Marxism,* Columbia University Press, New York, 1958.

heralded "end of ideology" and prevalence of pragmatic politics in Europe and America, though nowhere else, may well lead us to new ways of looking at our past in which the search for ideology plays a far less important part than it did in the preceding decades.[39] A greater interest in psychology may lead to far more refined and detailed ways of analyzing the history of ideas than the broad generalizations of the philosophies of history of the past century permitted. Indeed, with the new awareness of the complexity of social life the latter may soon lose their hold on the historical imagination altogether. As the label "the age of ideology" implies, nineteenth-century social thinking was in many ways entirely novel.[40] In its relentless future-directed, prophetic, activist and all-encompassing pretensions, its pseudoscientific aspirations and its dogmatic ways, the typical system of ideas of that century was quite unlike the political theory that preceded it. Whether it is sufficient to say that all the "isms" of the age—the various kinds of liberalism, conservatism, socialism, nationalism, and racism—were surrogate religions, appealing to men dislocated by the Industrial Revolution and the decline of traditional values, cannot be easily determined. Here too there are levels of quality. At their philosophic best, Mill, Hegel, and Marx offered a new and serious interpretation of society and of their age. What made the last century so evidently an "age of ideology" was the way in which political ideas became a part of the new forms of political combat that emerged after the French Revolution. These were but a part of the novel political institutions and forms of government in which the mobilization of public opinion and the organization of political parties and groups played so paramount a part. The unmasking of ideology belonged to that age and its typical political preoccupations–preoccupations that are not a part of the current political life of Europe and the United States. It should not be surprising that the study of the history of political ideas will now be reexamined and interpreted in terms more in keeping with the experiences of the post-ideological age. For this task, however, a full understanding of the thinking represented by the selections in this book is an essential requirement.

[39] See Daniel Bell, *The End of Ideology,* The Free Press of Glencoe, New York, 1960, for one who welcomes these changes, and Jean Meynaud, *Destin des Idéologies,* Etudes de Science Politique, Lausanne, 1961, for one who sees many dangers in them.

[40] E.g., Frederick M. Watkins, *The Age of Ideology: Political Thought, 1750 to the Present,* Prentice-Hall, Englewood Cliffs, N.J., 1964.

SELECTED BIBLIOGRAPHY

[In addition to works mentioned in the footnotes.]

Adorno, T. W., et al., *The Authoritarian Personality,* New York: Harper, 1950.

———, "Beitrag zur Ideologieenlehre," *Kölner Zeitschrift für Soziologie,* VI, 1954, pp. 360 ff.

Aron, Raymond, *The Opium of the Intellectuals,* trans. by Terence Kilmartin. New York: Doubleday & Co., 1957.

Beauvoir, Simone de, "La Pensée de Droite Aujourd'hui," *Les Temps Modernes,* X, 1955, pp. 1537 ff. and 2219 ff.

Bergman, Gustav, "Ideology," *Ethics,* LXI, 1951, pp. 205 ff.

Birnbaum, Norman, ed., "The Sociological Study of Ideology (1940–1960)," *Current Sociology,* IX, 1960.

Bloch, Ernst, *Das Prinzip Hoffnung,* Berlin: Aufbau-Verlag, 1954–1956.

Bottomore, T. B., "Some Reflections on the Sociology of Knowledge," *British Journal of Sociology,* VII, 1956, pp. 52 ff.

Burks, R. V., "A Concept of Ideology for Historians," *Journal of the History of Ideas,* X, 1949, pp. 183 ff.

Christie, Richard, and Jahoda, Marie, eds., *Studies in the Scope and Method of the "Authoritarian Personality,"* New York: The Free Press of Glencoe, 1954.

Cohn, Norman, *The Pursuit of the Millennium,* New York: Harper, 1961.

De Gré, Gerard, *Society and Ideology,* New York: Columbia University Book Store, 1943.

———, "The Sociology of Knowledge and the Problem of Truth," *Journal of the History of Ideas,* II, 1941, pp. 110 ff.

De Huszar, G. B., ed., *The Intellectuals,* New York: The Free Press of Glencoe, 1960.

De Man, Henry, *The Psychology of Socialism,* trans. by Eden and Cedar Paul, New York: Henry Holt & Co., 1927.

Gabel, Joseph, *La Fausse Conscience,* Paris: Editions de Minuit, 1962.

Geiger, Theodor, *Ideologie und Wahrheit.* Stuttgart–Wien: Humboldt-Verlag, 1953.

Gurian, Waldemar, "Totalitarian Religions," *Review of Politics,* XIV, 1952, pp. 3 ff.

Halpern, Ben, "'Myth' and 'Ideology' in Modern Usage," *History and Theory,* I, 1961, pp. 129 ff.

Hayek, F. A. von, ct al., *Capitalism and the Historians,* Chicago: Chicago University Press, 1960.

———, *The Counter-Revolution of Science,* New York: The Free Press of Glencoe, 1952.

———, "Socialism and the Intellectuals," *Chicago Law Review,* XVI, 1949, pp. 417 ff.

Hexter, J. H., *Reappraisals in History,* Evanston: Northwestern University Press, 1961.

Kecskemeti, Paul, "Ideology and Class Consciousness," *Modern Review,* III, 1949–1950, pp. 138 ff.

Lane, R. E., *Political Ideology,* New York: The Free Press of Glencoe, 1962.

Lichtheim, George, *Marxism,* London: Routledge & Kegan Paul, 1961.

Lukacz, George, *Geschichte und Klassenbewusstsein,* Berlin: Malik, 1923.

———, *Studies in European Realism,* New York: Grossett & Dunlap, 1964.

Macpherson, C. B., "The Deceptive Task of Political Theory," *The Cambridge Journal,* VII, 1954, pp. 560.

Mannheim, Karl, *Diagnosis of our Time,* New York: Oxford University Press, 1944.

———, *Essays on the Sociology of Culture,* ed. by Ernest Mannheim, London: Routledge & Kegan Paul, 1956.

———, *Essays on the Sociology of Knowledge,* ed. by Paul Kecskemeti, London: Routledge & Kegan Paul, 1952.

———, *Man and Society in an Age of Reconstruction,* trans. by Edward Shils, New York: Harcourt, Brace & World., 1950.

Maquet, J. J. P., *The Sociology of Knowledge,* trans. by J. F. Locke, Boston: Beacon Press, 1951.

Merton, Robert, *Social Theory and Social Structure,* New York, The Free Press of Glencoe, 1962.

Metzger, W. P., "Ideology and the Intellectual," *Philosophy of Science,* XVI, 1949, pp. 125 ff.

Mills, C. Wright, *The Sociological Imagination,* New York: Oxford University Press, 1959.

Myrdal, Gunner, *Values in Social Theory,* London: Routledge & Kegan Paul, 1958.

Oakeshott, Michael, *Rationalism in Politics,* New York: Basic Books, 1962.

Pareto, Vilfredo, *Les Systèmes Socialistes,* Paris: Giard, 1926.

Plessner, Helmuth, *Zwischen Philosophie und Gesellschaft,* Bern: Francke, 1953.

Popper, K. R., *The Poverty of Historicism,* Boston: Beacon Press, 1957.

Roucek, Joseph, "The History of the Concept of Ideology," *Journal of the History of Ideas,* V, 1944, pp. 480 ff.

Schumpeter, J. A., "Ideology and Politics," *American Economic Review,* XXXIX, 1949, pp. 345 ff.

———, *Social Classes and Imperialism,* New York: Meridian Books, 1955.
Shils, Edward, "Intellectuals and the Powers," *Comparative Studies in Society and History,* I, 1958, pp. 5 ff.
Sorel, Georges, *Reflections on Violence,* trans. by T. E. Hulme, New York: The Free Press of Glencoe, 1950.
Speier, Hans, *Social Order and the Risks of War,* New York: Stewart, 1952.
Wolff, K. H., ed., *The Sociology of Georg Simmel,* New York: The Free Press of Glencoe, 1950.
Ziegler, Hans, "Ideologieenlehre," *Archiv für Sozialwissenschaft und Sozialpolitik,* LVII, 1927, pp. 657 ff.

MACHIAVELLI AND THE END OF A BOURGEOIS CULTURE *

Alfred von Martin

Alfred von Martin is professor of sociology at the University of Munich. He was the author of several works on medieval and early modern intellectual history, based on the theories of both Dilthey and Mannheim, before the Nazis forced him into silence. Since 1945 he has written extensively about general sociology and the modern history of ideas.

As a rule the Renaissance is studied as a period of fine art and great intellects; this essay attempts to go behind these outward forms. It analyses the social realities which gave rise to this culture, in particular that class of "property and intellect" which here makes its first appearance in modern history; property is considered before the intellect, and in both cases the fateful intermediate position of this *haute bourgeoisie* between the aristocracy and the lower orders, the middle class and the proletariat has to be brought out. The cultural consequences of this intermediate position had to be traced through all the transformations which this society underwent in the process of its rise and decline. This

* Reprinted by permission of Routledge & Kegan Paul, Ltd., from Alfred von Martin, *The Sociology of the Renaissance,* translated by W. L. Luetkens, London: Kegan Paul, Trench, Trubner & Co., pp. lx, 3, 20–24, 32–33, 36–39, 65–69.

begins with the new impulses which the emerging bourgeoisie transmitted to all spheres of life and leads first to the cultural heights which were thus achieved and then down again to the point where the democratic régime which the *haute bourgeoisie* controlled entered upon its crisis and came to the verge of bankruptcy, a position which the contemporary Machiavelli clearly diagnosed from a proto-Fascist point of view. . . .

But for the sociologist the interest of the period lies in the fact that it presents him with the complete rhythmic progression of the ideal type of a cultural epoch dominated by the bourgeoisie. The differentiation of Early, Full and Late Renaissance, originally devised by the art critic, finds its sociological meaning in those social changes which are expressed in the stylistic ones. The prelude to the bourgeois era which we call the Renaissance begins in the spirit of democracy and ends in the spirit of the court. The first phase represents the rise of a few above the rest. This is followed by the securing of their newly won exalted position and the attempt to establish relations with the feudal aristocracy and to adopt their way of life. From the very beginning, that part of the bourgeoisie which gave its character to the period, i.e. the capitalist entrepreneurs, feels itself called upon to rule. In order to achieve this end it must first eliminate the former rulers on its "Right" by making an alliance with the "Left". But from the very beginning it has a tendency towards the "Right"; a tendency to intermix with the traditional ruling classes, to adopt their way of life, their attitude and their mode of thought and to attempt to become part of feudal "good" society.

The humanists—representatives of the intelligentsia—follow the same road and feel themselves tied to the new élite; whether this attachment was voluntary or no is of secondary importance here. Under the circumstances "democracy" meant no more than opposition to the privileges of the old powers, the clergy and the feudal nobility; hence the negation of those values which served to uphold their special position; it meant a new, bourgeois principle of selection according to purely individual criteria and not according to birth and rank. But liberty was not made into a revolutionary principle symbolizing an onslaught upon all and every established authority. In particular the Church was respected as an authoritative institution, and the only aim of the bourgeoisie was to vindicate its right to a position of importance. "A complete self-disarmament, such as the upper Estates carried through before the Revolution in France under the influence of Rousseau, was out of the question among these utilitarian Italians". This bourgeoisie of the Renaissance had a strong sense of what would enhance its power; its rationalism served it without ever endangering its position. . . .

Organization is based upon the conscious acts of individuals. But in order to act correctly the individual requires a knowledge of nature and its laws. Only when he possesses such knowledge can he master nature. Such practical learning is needed in order to work one's will. The ability to master the outside world gives the individual an opportunity to rise in the social scale. It is typical of the bourgeoisie and of the town and utterly alien to feudal and religious thought to believe that all things are possible and that the one necessary instrument is a rationa technique.

The new technique in its widest sense, whose unlimited applicatior constituted the new freedom of the individual, presupposed absolut laws of nature. And so, in the guise of the secular scientist, th bourgeois set about establishing the absoluteness of the laws of nature, which was required for his specific ends. The Middle Ages themselves had known the concept of laws of nature, but to them it was of secondary importance. In the semi-rational system of thought these laws were classed as *causae secundae;* above them was the metaphysical *causa primaria,* which thus constantly allowed for the possible interference of a divine miracle in the rational but secondary scheme of cause and effect. This latter, though it was ordained by God, was in fact always subject to interference. There was a supreme divine authority which disposed of the means of interference just as there was its representative on earth. The Church, i.e. the sacerdotal hierarchy, though it allowed secular life to go on according to its own laws, similarly reserved for itself a right of supreme control. This is no simple analogy in external appearances, but an inner, sociologically conditioned relation. It must of course not be understood in a vulgar materialist way as the conscious upholding of what was known to be a fiction in the interests of a social group, but as an unconscious formation of modes of thought by their indissoluble link with a particular set of social conditions. By analogy, the assignment of an absolute place to what had hitherto been *causae secundae* was the ideological reflection of the struggle for the emancipation of the bourgeoisie. This throwing off of clerical tutelage and this trend in ideas were one of its weapons, which was later adapted by the bourgeois engineer and technician to an immediately practical end. The concept of an absolute law in nature—and also in politics such as Machiavelli attempted to evolve—served in the struggle for bourgeois free competition. The fact that despite this development the concept of the divine rule of the world was not simply denied, that in fact it was assigned a kind of seat of honour, that the possibility of miracles was not ruled out but simply and silently ignored, was but a concession to decorum and not an admission that such possibilities actually existed. It is exactly parallel in the way in which the authority of the clergy and the Church was undermined but not directly attacked in polemic. It was regarded as "nonsensical" to enquire into "supra-natural things and things unseen" and "similar abyss-like mysteries", as Guicciardini put it. Only "natural" causes were considered and metaphysics ceased to hold interest. The world with which men were fitting themselves to deal had become a world without God. He might conceivably exist somewhere, but he was no longer a part of the world of the living as the Middle Ages had believed. God had been removed to another distant sphere, and bourgeois secular thought everywhere based itself upon practical experience, be it in the natural sciences of Leonardo or in the statecraft of Machiavelli.

Seen by the light of bourgeois empiricism as opposed to the speculation of the cleric and the clerical philosopher, the relations of the individual to the cosmos took on a completely different form. The development was to lead through Giordano Bruno to Galileo, in fact to a completely secularized attitude to the world from which all irrationalism has been expunged. It is the attitude of a type of individualistic intellectual entrepreneur, which truly corresponded to the new capitalist attitude in economic matters. Simmel actually discerns a causal relationship to the money economy.* "It is a money economy which for the first time created the ideal of exact numerical calculation"; the "mathematically exact interpretation of the cosmos" is the "theoretical counterpart of a money economy". This method of interpreting the world by a number of mathematical equations, without regard for the natural limitations on life of which one thought oneself independent, this way of regarding the world as one big arithmetical problem with absolutely impersonal, abstract, interchangeable and measurable quantities, presents a complete contrast to the more spontaneous and emotional attitude of

* Georg Simmel (1858–1918), German philosopher, historian and sociologist, was especially influential in introducing sociological concepts into the study of intellectual history.

the Middle Ages. Behind this attitude was the new will to power which it served, and which also contrasts with the completely different will to power prevalent in the previous age. In the Middle Ages this will had been predominantly political and directed towards the rule of men; the desire for dominion over "territories and things" existed only as a means towards "dominion over men". Parallel to the feudal will to power ran that of the clergy, the other ruling group of the times. Together they founded a system of rule which, on the material side, was originally based upon military power, which had become traditional, and on the spiritual side was based upon religious tradition. But when the old ruling groups were replaced by the bourgeoisie, the will to power took on different forms. It was now economic and technical, directed towards a "productive transformation of material things". No longer was the domination of men the end; man had become the instrument of domination. Only now we find the trend towards a thorough exploitation of human labour, which was declared "free" to this end. This was the great change from the Middle Ages, where every subordination implied the right to protection by one's lord. The new sciences and technical knowledge were the servants of the new will to economic power. Expressing as they did the new rational, liberal tendencies as opposed to the old conservative ones, they were also the immediate result of the new urge to intellectual power. The new money economy had given a new direction to the will to power, and a new kind of knowledge was ready to serve the bourgeoisie as a weapon in its struggle for emancipation and for power. Now, this quest for power took the form of a struggle for control over nature, based upon the understanding of its laws. In fact, even the new sciences were the outcome of the new spirit of enterprise, which was no longer prepared to put up with traditionally accepted but unexplained relationships of divine origin. It took all such relations to be capable of analysis by reason. This conception was applied not only theoretically to the methods of science, which now took nothing for granted, but also to the use of scientific knowledge. This was harnessed to immediately practical ends in the technical sciences which come easily to the bourgeois thinker, an engineer by nature. Knowledge was pursued with the aim of interfering in natural processes; one wanted to understand them in order to impose one's own power upon them. But only the new bourgeois, naturalist explanation of the world could give mastery over nature; it thus served the social function of ministering to the rising social group, and hence became predominant.

On the other hand, as Dilthey has pointed out, the natural sciences themselves were furthered by their close contact with industrial production.* The increasing practical needs which arose within bourgeois society, the new requirements of life, set problems which could be solved only by close co-operation between the practical worker and the scientific theorist, which expressed itself by experiment and calculation, by discovery and invention. The great scientists Ubaldi, Benedetti, Leonardo or Galileo set themselves tasks which arose from problems of navigation, shipbuilding or the construction of towns and fortifications. As firearms improved, war itself, which in the old days had been decided by cavalry battles, became increasingly a technical matter, and as artillery increased in importance, war became a task for the engineer. Men like Federigo of Urbino and Alfonso d'Este were representatives of the new type of military expert. We find a military science or art arising which subjected war to bourgeois influences. We find spectators who were not themselves involved "taking an objective pleasure in watching correct strategy for its own sake". There is an exact parallel to this in the equally rational science and technique of politics which called for a *virtuoso* of calculating intellect and expert talent, as described by Machiavelli. Even the ideas of the Ancients—rediscovered by the humanists—were made to serve military and political practice. As has already been suggested, the rise of the exact sciences was made possible by the intermixture of two social groups which had been separate. The intellectuals constituted one of these groups—men of practical experience in the crafts and in industry the other. The interest of the latter was involved because they were given the chance of improving their own practically acquired knowledge as well as their own social position. In this way the theoretical and the practical, technical approach joined hands in a community of work which was quite different from the mediaeval community of erudition. The *homo religiosus* of the Middle Ages had interpreted the world as a divine creation; the bourgeoisie of the Renaissance saw it as an object for human work and foresight, for human ordering and fashioning. The urge to domination and management conditioned the aims and methods of the

* Wilhelm Dilthey (1833–1911), German philosopher and historian, especially influential as a philosopher of history and cultural historian.

new sciences; the investigation of nature, engineering and industry gave them their character. . . .

The great majority of the humanists as well as of the artists came from bourgeois families, as was to be expected in view of the urban character of the new culture. Both the *haute bourgeoisie* and the new intellectuals worked their way up from the economic middle class. In the urban atmosphere where birth and Estate were no longer decisive, and where personal prestige was increasingly important, intellectual eminence too might be the means of improving one's place in society, and could thus have far-reaching social consequences, such as the replacement of clerics by laymen in urban education, in scientific, literary and artistic work. But although the laity supplanted the clergy in these fields, they made little attempt to establish "downward" contacts. On the contrary, they desired to fill the vacant position of an intellectual élite and of leadership over the uneducated. Thus a new social rift opened, no less wide than the economic rift which was the result of capitalism. Not only did the New Learning give the humanists an immense feeling of their own superiority (characteristically this was personal rather than corporate), but it gave them the halo of a strange prestige in the eyes of the despised πολλοι.* Classical learning was endowed with magic qualities similar to those attributed to the inexplicably rapidly acquired wealth of the capitalist, which appeared mysterious and almost sinister to the populace unable to understand how it had been won. In this way the people itself helped to make conscious the division between itself and the propertied and erudite classes.

Characteristic of and decisive for the structure of the intellectual élite was the diversity of its social origins. Petrarca, the first as well as the greatest of the humanists, began as an elegant young cleric at the Curia in Avignon. Boccaccio came from a family of merchants, and his patrimony gave him a life of moderate affluence. Until his father's death Niccolo Niccoli was active in trade, and Giannozzo Manetti was a banker's bookkeeper until he retired from business to devote himself to "his studies and to politics". In Florence a sequence of Secretaries to the Ten from Salutati to Machiavelli, and including men like Bruni, Poggio and Marsuppini, were humanists. This last group secured its material backing—and by its very nature an intermediary class such as the intelligentsia needs some sort of support to safeguard its existence —in a way natural to a bourgeois who still felt the pull of local ties. . . .

* πολλοι = polloi = people, populace.

Any politico-economic ruling class has a corresponding intellectual leading group, arising from the same social situation. The intellectual leading group supports the power position of the ruling class by the provision of an ideology and by guiding public opinion in the requisite direction. The function had been fulfilled in the Middle Ages by the clerical intellectuals; now it devolved upon the humanists. The former were the type of auxiliary required for rule by tradition, the latter were the pacemakers for a rational or "charismatic" rule. In a conservative world, based on static existence, religion was the adjunct of politics because of its emphatic upholding of tradition; equally, in a liberal world, stressing exclusively activity and achievement, science and work, which both aim at the expansion of existing scope, belong together. One age was relatively static, the other to a large degree dynamic and "progressive". In the former an existing ruling class attempted to perpetuate its power and possessions; in the other, forces and abilities which previously had been shackled were vigorously breaking out.

Blood, i.e. the privilege of birth, and the sacerdotal consecration had been the principles of selection of the mediaeval ruling class. The new criteria were those of wealth and erudition. Priest and feudal noble were displaced from their hegemony by the new economic power of money and the indirect beneficiary of the power of money, the independent intellect; their place was taken by the alliance of bourgeois and humanist. Both were in direct opposition to the supra-rational modes of thought of the priest and the knight which ignored economic matters as well as the new intellectualism. Above all they swung away from that chivalry whose fundamental categories, courage and honour, ran directly counter to the calculating spirit of the bourgeois; ecclesiastical thought, by nature more elastic, was able to become rational in the Renaissance, though it was forced largely to abandon its spiritual character. Money and talent were forced together in face of mediaeval tradition; they met on common ground, as the typically bourgeois spirit of calculation and of rationally adapting means to ends are a characteristic of both the merchant and the intellectual: the new powers were akin in spirit as well as by choice. They were filled with the spirit of enterprise which produced similar attitudes, regardless of the fact that they applied it in the one case to economic and in the other to intellectual matters, two fields which have but little in common. . . .

Money and intellect: these were the two great motive powers in the rise of those whose birth put them at a social disadvantage. *"Extolle te* *super homines!*"—already in the case of Salutati this was the real foundation of humanist study.* A whole generation earlier Petrarca had known how to put this into practice, and later the ability or at any rate the will to stand out among men was common to all humanists. Aeneas Sylvius is responsible for its sharpest formulation: "Knowledge . . . which . . . causes the learned to stand out above the unlearned makes the former like unto God . . . even those of the most humble origin it lifts to the level of the greatest." It should be remembered that the humanists, or at any rate the greatest among them, at least in theory (though frequently not in their mode of life) consciously upheld definite values. But the inherent tendency of Humanism—though not all humanists realized this—was characterized by the fact that already with Salutati the central concept of *virtus* began to lose its moral context and became increasingly formalized. More and more it came to mean intellectual *studium,* thus coming into line with the equally formal *virtù,* signifying initiative and ability, and all forms of dynamic striving by the individual. . . .

There is always one danger for those who occupy the highest position: that the limit of ascent may be reached, that progress may cease and that there may remain no possibility of a continued upward development. Moreover, there is an added danger in the free disposition over all means: the dynamic enticement towards new goals may be stifled by the perfected manipulation of mere technique. In all fields, economic as well as cultural, political as well as artistic, a perfected virtuosity had been achieved and with it a certain static had intervened. The question could be asked whether *virtù,* an important element of which was activist energy, had not been buried under this ubiquitous virtuosity. This was the problem of Machiavelli. He, in a handbook of statecraft, gave a compendium of all the political methods of his day; and yet his constant eager quest after *virtù* shows us the great shortcoming of these shifts and devices, and thus indicates the nature of the crisis of his times.

Machiavelli was a man who stood opposed to the spirit of his day; he mercilessly criticized his times, whose weaknesses were patent to his penetrating eye. A sixteenth-century parallel to Oswald Spengler,† he saw that bourgeois civilization had seen its spring and summer, that

* "Raise yourself above men."

† Oswald Spengler (1880–1936), author of the celebrated *The Decline of the West* and other works on modern civilization.

autumn had come and that winter was drawing near. It was this tragic cycle which to him was the fundamental law of all history; he saw it in the story of Greece and Rome and again in the course of his own contemporary Renaissance. As the goal of endeavour is successfully achieved security comes, leading to "slackening and effeminacy" and thus to decay and ruin. To him the security of the bourgeois was his decisive danger; it was a sign of decadence, and Machiavelli, who turned against everything which his contemporaries valued most, confronted them with his own vexatious philosophy. He was bitterly opposed to the idealization of prosperity as well as to the refined leisure of a humanist and artistic culture. These static ideals had exposed the bourgeoisie, once a powerfully rising class, to a comfortable complacency wary of sacrifice; thus *virtù* had decayed in its genuine dynamic meaning of *forza,* whose final expression was in war. Humanism had promised to raise men above a brutish state without culture and reason, and thus really to make them into men, but it achieved nothing beyond making them into *"bons bourgeois"*. Far better if man were to return to the simplicity of his "brutish" existence, to the ideal of a primitive state of nature; far better if the rich and cultured bourgeois were to become once again a poor but warlike peasant! Just as Tacitus held up the Germans as a model to decadent Rome, Machiavelli pointed to the Swiss: they were a people of simple manners and life, an armed people and a real democracy. The national democrat pointed to the bankruptcy of bourgeois liberalism and announced the political failure of private capitalism. The money economy of the merchants had undermined the soldierly qualities.

Overland commerce, in contrast to maritime commerce, is by its nature not bellicose but purely mercantile in character, inclined to peaceful trading and bargaining. The militant self-confidence which gave strength to the inland communes in their heroic periods was a Teutonic heritage going back to the castles and the free peasant communities of Lombard days. But the urban air, above all of Florence, where bankers became princes, overlaid it with bourgeois characteristics. Alberti's exemplary bourgeois and urban outlook belies completely the aristocratic blood of his warlike ancestors. He himself explained the outstanding business abilities of his compatriots by pointing out that they were able to devote themselves to this avenue to the exclusion of all others and were able to specialize completely, because they had no need for any sort of military training. War could be left to the mercenaries, and even the door to political prominence was unlocked by monetary wealth which had to be earned in business. Petrarca in his *Familiar Letters* wrote: *"Qui divites sunt, boni viri in civitatibus appellantur eisque tantum creditur."* * Reversing the mediaeval situation, economic assumed primacy over political matters—and thus also "reason" asserted itself over that passion which is prepared to go to war, for reason, left to itself, wants peace. In this manner the mercantile spirit got the better of warlike inclinations; the idea of universal military training was lost and the "bourgeois" type arose with all its unmilitary virtues. Florentine statesmen were able to praise "freedom" itself for its usefulness; the highest political ideal was judged by its utility value. Everything, including war, was regarded as business by the bourgeoisie. The multitude disarmed itself, accomplishing of its own free will what was usually the first act of a despotism after it had triumphed over the bourgeoisie. The citizen gave pride of place to the bourgeois. No longer able to fight, the bourgeoisie accepted as inevitable and normal pressure from above and maintained but the ideal of a private economic or humanist freedom; a freedom from interference by the state.

Machiavelli saw himself face to face with this situation, and he clearly grasped the interconnection of politics and economic matters as well as the antinomies between the common weal and the interests of the individual. In politics and war, so he thought, one should not forget the importance of economic power; the state must be rich in order to make full use of its power as a state. But could one call "the state" rich if it had a rich bourgeoisie? On the one hand, so he answered, the wealth of so many was a source of Florentine power, and he thought that one of the advantages of the free democratic town was that in it individual wealth was more easily increased; on the other hand, with wealth comes the danger of corruption, so that the blessing seemed a mixed one at best. Wealth militates against the *virtù* of individual and state alike; it impairs military prowess and thus the state becomes unable to defend itself. In the last resort, so he thought, the power of the state is the armed power vested in a militia. Italy was already threatened by foreign domination and the capitalist economy and capitalist policy had not been found sufficient in the struggle for power. So he argued that poor citizens serve the state better than rich: let

* "Those who are rich are reputed to be good men in the cities, and they are the only ones who are trusted."

them be poor and prepare for war. Let them be different from those "pure" merchants who live for the "philosophy of money", from whose calculating point of view egoism alone is logical and all "devotion and sacrifice" born of the irrational forces of emotion and desire are only the "proof of a lack of wisdom" and the butt of irony. This bourgeois onesidedness and specialization was the key to the rise of bourgeois civilization, but it already contained the seeds of its decline and ruin. The exaggerated valuation of business and of the mind, of reason and taste, had created a race which was bound to succumb in the struggle for political survival.

Now that the battle for survival or death had come, these "pale" bourgeois spirits of the type of Piero Soderini could talk of nothing but their bourgeois compromises "which are always harmful"; for them even hell was too good: they belonged to the *limbo dei bambini.** And, according to Machiavelli, such bourgeois policies with their soft, pacifistic and antiheroic ideal corresponded to a morality which had been nursed by Christianity; not indeed the original Christianity of Christ but its degenerate clerical form. Ecclesiastical Christianity with its emphasis on the Beyond and on humility had helped to paralyse all love of liberty and all political energy, thereby working hand in hand with the mercantile interests. Thus traditional Christian and ecclesiastical morality had only worked against the necessary power policy of the state, putting into its place the clerical and by now empty though high-sounding ideology of the *optimus princeps* and the *rex instus* who should be good and just, in the sense and interest desired by the Church.† Against such an embellishing idealism Machiavelli's realistic honesty reacted with the desire for its complete destruction.

Machiavelli's dislike of clericalism was matched by his hatred of feudalism. Those nobles who devoted themselves to trade as the most profitable and respected calling that their ancestral town could offer, as they did at Venice and Florence, were in his eyes no longer members of the aristocracy; he regarded as the feudal type proper those nobles who in "idleness" and "abundance" lived off unearned rents. Machiavelli still maintained enough of the dislike of the early bourgeois, the *civis,* for the aristocracy, to desire its exile or extermination, because idleness and abundance were harmful to the state. He saw that the nobility had lost its function in a transformed society and in a new war-

* *The limbo of babes.*

† *The best ruler* and *the just king.*

fare, which was no longer based upon the arm of the well-to-do, the cavalry, but upon the foot soldier.

And so Machiavelli sought a common denominator for his anti-mercantile as well as his anti-clerical and anti-feudal convictions. He found it in a new humanist ideology, the myth of the *antica virtù,* the *virtù Romana.* The easy-going, static thought of men in the line of Sadoleto and Petrarca took as its ideal the philosophic rentierdom of a decadent late classical period; now it had become necessary to arouse Italy from this slumber. According to the habits of thought of his time, which looked upon Antiquity as the model in all things, Machiavelli projected backwards his ideal of dynamic energy and driving power to which he had been led by criticizing his own times. There he came upon the as yet unspoilt and simple Rome of the early Republic. This was a time when a vigorous paganism was as yet far from being ousted by an individualist, cosmopolitan humanist philosophy. To Machiavelli this paganism was an active source of strength to the state, whereas he was never able to come to anything more than an opportunist relationship with Christianity and with the Church.

The consciousness of the decadence of his own day drove Machiavelli to the romantic idea of a rebirth of this *virtù Romana* in a "Third Reich". Against the threatening foreign conquest there was not even the will to resist: *"materia corrotta"* was his complaint.* But, so he thought the masses are never more than a rabble, and it is only the leader who matters. "Great men make history", the masses follow. The "rebirth" had to be brought about by a dictator, one who shall arise from the "obscurity of a lowly position" to bring about *"grandissime cose"* † as one of the elect of *fortuna* and of that "god who befriends the strong"; he shall be such as was Castruccio, the despot of Lucca, whose personality Machiavelli exalted to such an ideal.

Free of all traditional ethical norms he shall bring about the miracle of salvation by means of *virtù* only and with but one obligation: that of success. The miracle to be achieved was no less than that of winning freedom and unity for Italy by force of arms. In these romantic flights Machiavelli came precariously near to Petrarca the poet and dreamer; his romanticism was the romanticism of Reason; the belief that by means of skilful organization everything could be compassed became

* *Corrupt material.*
† *Really great things.*

a superstition, a caricature of *Realpolitik*. It was the last, desperate and already half-resigned cry of the "last free bourgeois."

THOMAS HOBBES AND THE REVOLUTION IN POLITICAL THOUGHT *

Christopher Hill

Christopher Hill is a Fellow and Tutor in Modern History at Balliol College in Oxford. He is a leading authority on seventeenth century England, and especially its religious history, and he has written extensively about it, including a comprehensive account of the age, The Century of Revolution 1603–1714 *(Edinburgh: Nelson, 1961). He is also the author of a book on Lenin.*

Thomas Hobbes was born in 1588 and lived till 1679. His life thus extends from the defeat of the Spanish Armada to the beginning of the Popish Plot; from the year in which the independence of Protestant England was finally ensured to the period when a threat to restore Catholicism in England was less a political reality than the stunt of a Parliamentary party. The Revolution of 1640 occurred after Hobbes was 50 years old, when his main ideas had taken form. But they had been shaped by the intellectual forces of his world.

Hobbes was, as Aubrey put it, "of plebeian descent". His father was a country vicar, and by all accounts not a very learned one. But he died while Thomas was still young, and . . . the boy's education was financed by his uncle, in this case a prosperous glover and alderman of Malmesbury. His mother came of yeoman stock. They managed to send him to Oxford. From there he passed in 1608 into the service of the great family of the Cavendishes, as tutor to the future Earl of

* Reprinted by permission of Schocken Books, Inc. from *Puritanism and Revolution* (London: Secker & Warburg, pp. 275–291), by Christopher Hill. Copyright © 1958 by Christopher Hill. Published in England by Martin Secker & Warburg, Ltd., and used with their permission.

Devonshire. At one period—we do not know exactly when—Hobbes worked in close collaboration with Bacon, acting as his amanuensis. But with brief interruptions he remained in the service of the Cavendish family until 1640, when he fled to Paris and the Cavendishes began to gather an army for Charles I. In Paris, Hobbes was for a time tutor to Prince Charles. In 1653, after his return to England, Hobbes resumed his service with the Cavendish family.

Like many of the great landed families, the Cavendishes were in financial difficulties. "His lord", says Aubrey delicately, "was a waster"; and Hobbes wore out his shoes and got colds from wet feet by being sent "up and downe to borrow money and gett gentlemen to be bound" for the second Earl of Devonshire.[1] Hobbes taught the Earl to keep accounts; but nevertheless his extravagance brought disaster on the family. After his death in 1628 Hobbes was out of the family's employment for three years whilst the widow was trying to restore some sort of economic order. So the glover's nephew learnt something of the economic hazards as well as of the external splendour of a feudal ruling house.

The contradiction is apparent. Hobbes, the small bourgeois, the clever boy making good at Oxford, is taken into the service of one of the most conservative of the great feudal families which still ruled large tracts of the economically backward north of England. When Hobbes takes his noble pupils on the grand tour of Europe he meets the most advanced intellects of his time—Galileo, Descartes, Gassendi. He comes home to discuss their ideas with the Duke of Newcastle.

Hobbes's station in the world thus rendered him conscious of conflict, of the rifts in society which were plunging it into a civil war that would be fatal to his position as a hanger-on of the old order. In *Behemoth* he gives a convincing social analysis of the causes of the Civil War. In the *De Cive* and *Leviathan* his object is to prevent that conflict (or any other conflict) ever taking the extreme form of civil war. Hobbes's theory of sovereignty dates from the actual period of armed conflict in England.

So Hobbes, suspended between two worlds, is equally critical of both. His environment and mode of life may have aligned him with the old order politically, but none can deny the revolutionariness of his method, of his criticism, the boldness of his rejections. Even his reasons for rejecting revolutionary Puritanism have far-reaching implications:

[1] Aubrey, *Brief Lives*, I, pp. 322–3, 347.

for his critical-sceptical approach cut right through the religious smoke screen which concealed divisions within the ranks whilst seventeenth-century Parliaments advanced on power.

What then was the Hobbesian revolution?

Hobbes found official political thought dominated by the idea that government was to be obeyed because ordained of God; and he substituted the theory that the state was instituted by man for his own convenience, and that it should be obeyed because the consequences of disobedience can be demonstrated to be more disagreeable than obedience, in almost all cases. That is to say, expediency, not morality, is for Hobbes the motive for political obedience.

Hobbes found opposition thinking dominated by the idea that government should not be obeyed when it conflicted with divine law, natural law, natural rights; and he showed that natural law, morality, and rights in society are derived from the state, and that it is nonsense to speak of "natural rights" antecedent to the state, just as it is impossible to obtain agreement among men on what constitutes divine, natural, or fundamental law except in so far as these have been defined by the sovereign. That is to say, he made power, not right, the key question in politics.

Finally, Hobbes abandoned the old games of text swapping and precedent hunting for logical argument. That is to say, he made reason, not authority, the arbiter in politics. Paradoxically, it is the absolutist Hobbes who demonstrated that the state exists for man, that it is the product of human reason, and therefore that political theory is a rational science.

Despite his practical conclusions, then, the whole essence of Hobbes's approach to politics, his mental atmosphere and presuppositions, are "bourgeois". He postulates a society in which traditional static hierarchical feudal relations have broken down. In the mediaeval state the important questions had been those of personal status and privilege the relation of lord to serf, of guild member to purchaser, of cleric to layman. But by the seventeenth century, society has dissolved into its component parts, who face one another not as members of estates or corporations but as egoistic individuals. This new individualism is reflected in religion: Hobbes's view of human nature is that of Calvinism or Jansenism; he has as little use as Calvin for the hierarchy of saints, the mediating priesthood, the round of formal "works" by which the mediaeval Catholic hoped to save his soul. Hobbes sees society as a collection of atoms, in which the important relations are contractual, such as those between employer and workman, the Nonconformist and the minister whom he selects: the emphasis is on the individual, not on the social group. Hobbes's natural man is an individualist, like Robinson Crusoe or Adam Smith's economic man. Like Descartes, Hobbes believes he can generalize about the passions of all men by examining his own. His state is a mechanical contrivance, set up by contract. The contract idea which he adopts was almost the private property of the Puritan and revolutionary opposition, whether we consider the *Vindiciae contra Tyrannos,** which was the Bible of the Dutch revolutionaries and the French Huguenots, the covenant theology of John Preston, or the Solemn League and Covenant which bound together the Scottish and English opponents of Charles I.

Hobbes postulates the complete equality of natural man in "the faculties of body and mind". "The inequality that now is, has bin introduced by the Lawes civill." [2] "Good Counsell comes not by Lot, nor by Inheritance; and therefore there is no more reason to expect good Advice from the rich, or noble, in matter of State, than in delineating the dimensions of a fortresse." So the sovereign will give the hereditary aristocracy "no further honour, than adhaereth naturally to their abilities." [3] No egalitarian democrat could go further. How right Clarendon was to upbraid Hobbes for "his extreme malignity to the Nobility, by whose bread he hath bin alwaies sustain'd." The noble lord correctly pointed out that the Levellers concurred with Hobbes's view "that no man may have privileges of that kind by his birth or descent".[4]

Man in the state of nature, for Hobbes, is an abstraction from the competitive world he saw about him: the fittest survive. Indeed, he goes out of his way to tell us that his state of nature is a logical abstraction rather than a piece of historical description.[5] Natural man is "bourgeois" man with the policeman removed. The main objections which Hobbes makes to his state of nature are such as would occur to

* A treatise, of uncertain authorship that appeared in 1579 and set forth a Calvinist justification for rebellion against rulers who violated their principal obligations to God and man.

[2] *Leviathan* (Everyman ed.), pp. 63, 79.

[3] *Ibid.*, pp. 187–8.

[4] Clarendon, *A Brief View and Survey*, pp. 181–2. Cf. p. 211 above.

[5] *Leviathan*, p. 65.

and appeal to the commercial classes: "There is no place for Industry; because the fruit thereof is uncertain: and consequently no Culture of the Earth, no Navigation, nor use of the commodities that may be imported by Sea; no commodious Building; no Instruments of moving, and removing such things as require much force; no Knowledge of the face of the Earth; no account of Time; no Arts; no Letters; no Society." [6] The setting up of the sovereign state is the only escape from the natural state of war: [7] but it also alone makes possible any of the achievements of civilization.

Man emerges from the state of nature by his own efforts, by self-help based on the use of reason. The laws of nature are "precepts or general rules, found out by reason", and they lead to the elevation of the sovereign to save men from the state of war which is at once the state of nature and the condition of "feudal anarchy". "To seek peace and ensue it" is for Hobbes the first law of nature, the clue to all success in politics; and peace, internal order, and security are the first necessities of existence for the commercial and industrial classes.

The overriding problem of seventeenth-century politics, which Hobbes was shrewd enough to see absolutely clearly, was, Who was to interpret conflicting customs—King or Parliament, Lords or Commons? The House of Commons represented the landed class; but since capitalism in England was largely rural, many M.P.s in the seventeenth century had an outlook very different from that of the government. As the Crown, in its financial extremity, resorted to arbitrary taxation, so the House of Commons, to protect property, resurrected the claims of fifteenth-century Parliaments to a say in control of policy. There were therefore conflicting precedents with which the conflicting claims could be supported. Most students of politics devoted themselves to antiquarian research to find arguments for their own side, or to the hopeless task of discovering which side was "right". Hobbes brushed all these cobwebs aside, and showed that such questions were not decided by "right" but by power; what mattered was not arguments, but who was to decide between them. Custom, precedents, admittedly could produce contradictory conclusions: very well, then, the only important

[6] *Leviathan,* pp. 64–5. Cf. p. 89, and *The Elements of Law,* pp. 79–80.

[7] It leads, of course, to wars between states; but the state of nature is worse than the condition of warfare between nations, which may indeed be profitable to rulers: "But because they uphold thereby, the Industry of their Subjects; there does not follow from it, that misery, which accompanies the Liberty of particular men" (*Leviathan,* p. 65).

question was, Who was to interpret conflicting customs? This is the historical point of Hobbes's theory of sovereignty.

Hobbes agrees with almost all contemporary political theorists in seeing the rise of private property from a previously existing state of primitive communism as the cause and justification of the state. "For before constitution of Soveraign Power . . . all men had right to all things; which necessarily causeth Warre: and therefore this Proprietie, being necessary to Peace, and depending on Soveraign Power, is the Act of that Power, in order to the publique peace." [8] As property is inherited, and we may not go behind possession (sanctified by the sovereign) to question *right,* so sovereignty itself passes by inheritance, and we have no right to question the arrangements made by our ancestors. Sovereignty and property stand or fall together, are maintained by the same laws of inheritance.

Here again Hobbes is transitional, and this part of his argument seems the weakest in the light of later and more sophisticated contractual theories. But we must remember when and for whom Hobbes wrote. A society which believed that all men inherited the consequences of Adam's sin, and that Anglo-Saxon precedent was relevant to its own problems, could hardly boggle at an original contract which bound posterity. Hobbes's combination of contract and inheritance would make sense to a seventeenth-century landowner, for whom an unchallengeable succession of property is the important thing. It is only after the new standards have triumphed that even land loses its feudal status and becomes a commodity, which can be bought, sold, and devised, and is secured by contract. This development is reflected in political theory by the transition from divine hereditary right to Locke's contractually limited monarchy. Hobbes is writing at an intervening stage, and his arguments are addressed to the contractualists, to those, like Selden, who held that "a King is a thing men have made for their owne sakes, for quietness sake".[9] There is already nothing divine about the sovereign's right: that is why Hobbes was so unpopular with the high-flying Church of England men.

Hobbes is also a spokesman of the new attitude towards poverty in capitalist society. The idea that poverty was a holy state had long been abandoned. Opinion was now shifting away from the sixteenth-century view that pauperism should be dealt with by Christian charity.

[8] *Ibid.,* p. 93. For primitive communism, see *English Works,* II, p. vi.
[9] John Selden, *Table Talk* (1927), p. 61.

That solution had been sufficient for the occasional victims of misfortune in the more static mediaeval society: it could not cope with the mass unemployment created by early capitalism and enclosure of arable lands for sheep farming. Hobbes saw that pauperism on the new scale was a problem for the state. "And whereas many men, by accident unevitable, become unable to maintain themselves by their labour; they ought not to be left to the Charity of private persons; but to be provided for, (as far-forth as the necessities of Nature require), by the Lawes of the Common-wealth." But even this subsistence minimum must not be rashly distributed. "For such as have strong bodies, the case is otherwise: they are to be forced to work; and to avoyd the excuse of not finding employment, there ought to be such Lawes, as may encourage all manner of Arts: as Navigation, Agriculture, Fishing, and all manner of Manifacture that requires labour." Emigration is also a remedy for unemployment. And with Malthus, Hobbes concludes: "And when all the world is overcharged with Inhabitants, then the last remedy of all is Warre; which provideth for every man, by Victory, or Death." [10] The function of the state in a competitive world, as Hobbes sees it, is the mercantilist one of building up power for wealth and wealth for power, and building up power and wealth for ultimate war, the final arbiter of wealth and power.

One final point about the contract. "Whatsoever is not Unjust, is Just", says Hobbes. "And the definition of INJUSTICE, is no other than the *not Performance of Covenant*." [11] Justice is the keeping of contracts: no more. One consequence of this will be clear to anyone who is acquainted with the social problems of sixteenth- and seventeenth-century England. The burning question of the day was the position of the small proprietor, the copyholder or cottager, whose holding was frequently an obstacle to consolidation of estates, enclosure, racking of rents, and all the familiar methods by which one section of the gentry was enriching itself and sharing in the commercial and industrial boom of the century before 1640. The attack on the security of tenure of these small men, the mere idea that customary rents could be raised and that peasants unable to pay might be evicted, had seemed in the sixteenth century a breach with all that was right and proper, a gross violation of equity even when the letter of the law was observed. For most copyholders and cottagers held by customary right, at customary rents, not

[10] *Leviathan*, p. 185. Cf. pp. 215–38 above.
[11] *Ibid.*, p. 74; cf. *The Elements of Law*, pp. 63–5.

automatically enforceable at common law. There was no contractual basis for their claims. The aim of the improving landlord was to replace copyholds by leaseholds, copyholds for lives by copyholds for a fixed term of years; to substitute precise, limited, and determinable contracts for the indeterminate, traditional, customary right of the mediaeval peasantry; to pass from status to contract. It had been a moral as well as an economic revolution, an intrusion of the alien standards of the market into a sphere hitherto unaffected by them.

By the middle of the seventeenth century, no doubt, the new morality of competition was becoming generally accepted. The last attempt to legislate against depopulating enclosures was defeated in Parliament in 1656. But the peasants' struggle for stable copyholds still went on, supported by the Leveller movement just before the publication of *Leviathan*. The last pamphlets against enclosure were published in the 'fifties. At least the new standards were regarded as a lapse from the old, a concession to the wicked covetousness of fallen man. But now here was Hobbes making contract the basis of morality! Justice is the keeping of covenants: no contract, no injustice. Nowhere is the fundamentally "bourgeois" nature of Hobbes's approach to the state and to morality more apparent than in this, the foundation of both.

It should be noted, moreover, that though the basis is *contractual*, force is needed too to maintain contracts. Contracts are free, but must be maintained by force against the unfortunate. As that good Hobbist, Commissary-General Ireton, put it four years before the publication of *Leviathan:* "Any man that makes a bargaine, and does finde afterwards 'tis for the worse, yett is bound to stand to itt." "They were couzen'd", replied the Leveller Wildman, "as wee are like to be".[12]

The "bourgeois" characteristics of Hobbes's thought come out perhaps most clearly in his attitude to the Roman Church, and to non-rational elements in religion altogether. The point of the attack on the Kingdom of Darkness in Part IV of *Leviathan* is that Hobbes is defending the negative achievements of the Reformation, its break with priestcraft, its denial of the need for a hierarchy to mediate between man and God.

[12] *Clarke Papers* (ed. Firth, 1891–1901), II, p. 404. An enclosure agreement drawn up in 1702 by the freeholders of Eyam is an excellent example of a Hobbist contract: see W. E. Tate, "Enclosure Acts and Awards relating to Derbyshire", in *Derbyshire Archaeological and Natural History Society's Journal* (1944–5), pp. 63–4.

In the first three decades of the seventeenth century, in opposition to pressure from the Puritans, the Church of England under Lancelot Andrewes and Laud had reverted to a kind of social Papistry. With no desire to return to the Papal allegiance, such men wished to elevate the dignity of the priest, to distinguish him from the mass of the congregation, to emphasize the formal and symbolic aspects of worship (prayer and the sacraments) as against the rational (preaching). "There should be more praying, and less preaching", said Hobbes's patron, the Duke of Newcastle; "for much preaching breeds faction, but much praying causes devotion".[13] Hobbes had no love for Puritanism, for he held that the logical conclusion of its belief in the rights of the individual conscience was complete anarchy; but he was far too imbued with the new science to have any truck with the neo-Papist movement. In Part IV of *Leviathan* he is attacking "ghost" ideas, in Ibsen's sense of the word; clearing away impediments to rational thought. He openly contrasts religion with science. He mercilessly attacks superstition and belief in magic, for the specific reason that they are the means by which priests establish their authority over the people. "Who will not obey a Priest, that can make God, rather than his Soveraign; nay than God himselfe? Or who, that is in fear of Ghosts, will not bear great respect to those that can make Holy Water, that drives them from him?"[14] Claims to inspiration may be a cheat; and at best fear of hell and hopes of heaven are unsatisfactory as motives for political action.[15]

Hence Hobbes's Erastianism, which is as great as that of the majority of the House of Commons in 1640. The state must wield the vast power over men's minds which religion still possesses, just because of the infinite possibilities of disagreement and dispute which there would otherwise be. For "the most frequent praetext of Sedition, and Civill Warre, in Christian Common-wealths hath a long time proceeded from a difficulty, not yet sufficiently resolved, of obeying at once, both God, and Man, then when their Commandements are one contrary to the other".[16] It is in fact the question of sovereignty. Who is to decide? In the last resort, Hobbes thinks this is a question of power. The quarrel between the Puritans and Laud was only in appearance over doctrinal niceties, the position of the communion table, the priestly vestments.

[13] Duchess of Newcastle, *Lives of William Cavendish, Duke of Newcastle, and His Wife, Margaret,* ed. Firth, p. 124.

[14] *Leviathan,* p. 369.

[15] *Ibid.,* p. 76.

[16] *Ibid.,* p. 319.

In fact two philosophies of life were in conflict, two social orders: the mediaeval, the Catholic, the hierarchic, the feudal; and the modern, the Protestant-rationalist, the individualist, the bourgeois.

Yet whilst attacking the priesthood Hobbes has a clear perception of the uses of religion for keeping the vulgar in order. The ancient Romans "obtayned in order to their end, (which was the peace of the Common-wealth), that the common people in their misfortunes, laying the fault on neglect, or errour in their Ceremonies, or on their own disobedience to the lawes, were the less apt to mutiny against their Governors. And being entertained with the pomp, and pastime of Festivalls, and publike Games, made in honour of the Gods, needed nothing else but bread, to keep them from discontent, murmuring, and commotion against the state." [17]

Hobbes's definition of religion sufficiently indicates his view of its purpose, and his own complete Erastianism: "*Feare* of power invisible, feigned by the mind, or imagined from tales publiquely allowed, RELIGION; not allowed, SUPERSTITION. And [with a blatantly cynical nod to the decencies] when the power imagined, is truly such as we imagine, TRUE RELIGION." Religion, in fact, is an instrument of government, "In all things not contrary to the Morall Law, (that is to say, to the Law of Nature), all Subjects are bound to obey that for divine Law, which is declared to be so, by the Lawes of the Commonwealth." "An opinion publiquely appointed to bee taught, cannot be Haeresie; nor the Soveraign Princes that authorize them, Haeretiques." [18] The calmness with which Hobbes describes on paper and rationalizes the practice of all governments in his day takes one's breath away. He alone had the courage to justify the *cujus regio ejus religio* principles on which every government acted.*

It is not surprising, therefore, that the great enemy for Hobbes is the claim to inspiration, to direct revelation, to be able to work miracles. Here he is attacking the sectaries on the left as well as the Papists on the right; and in the process his rigorous logic undermines the whole Christian position. "To say [God] hath spoken to him in a Dream, is no more than to say he dreamed that God spake to him. . . . So that though God Almighty can speak to a man, by Dreams, Visions, Voice, and Inspiration; yet he obliges no man to beleeve he hath so done to

[17] *Ibid.*, pp. 59–60.
[18] *Ibid.*, pp. 26, 153, 316.
* Subjects must accept the religion of their ruler.

him that pretends it; who (being a man) may erre, and (which is more) may lie." "All the Miracle consisteth in this, that the Enchanter has deceived a man; which is no Miracle, but a very easie matter to doe. . . . For two men conspiring, one to seem lame, the other to cure him with a charme, will deceive many: but many conspiring, one to seem lame, another so to cure him, and all the rest to bear witnesse; will deceive many more." [19] Hobbes denies possession by devils, even in those cases where the devil was cast out by Christ. He also denies the existence of a local hell or everlasting torment.[20]

It is quite clear, in fact, that Hobbes does not really believe in Christianity, in any normal sense of the word "belief", and merely accepts it as the creed authorized in the state in which he lived.[21] "It was . . . almost impossible for man without the special assistance of God, to avoid both rocks of atheism and superstition." [22] God saves the situation by direct revelation; but we have already seen how dubious Hobbes is about claims to revelation as such. He is no Pascal, using scepticism to build up a firmer faith; he uses the existence of faith to inculcate scepticism. "Shall whole Nations", he asks, "be brought to *acquiesce* in the great Mysteries of Christian Religion, which are above Reason; and millions of men be made believe, that the same Body may be in innumerable places, at one and the same time, which is against Reason", and shall it be impossible to educate them into the more sensible principles of the Leviathan? [23]

Hobbes sneers at arguments based only on biblical texts. Those who employ them "by casting atomes of Scripture, as dust before men's eyes, make every thing more obscure than it is; an ordinary artifice of those that seek not the truth, but their own advantage".[24] He develops his own case by logic and rational demonstration first, then proceeds to bolster it up by texts, "with submission nevertheless both in this, and in all questions, whereof the determination dependeth on the Scriptures, to the interpretation of the Bible authorized by the Common-wealth, whose Subject I am".[25] Individual interpretation of the scriptures, carried to its logical conclusion, means as many truths and schemes of

[19] *Ibid.*, pp. 200, 238–9.
[20] *Ibid.*, pp. 244, 342, 351.
[21] *Ibid.*, p. 241.
[22] *English Works,* II, p. 227.
[23] *Leviathan,* p. 180.
[24] *Ibid.*, p. 329.
[25] *Ibid.*, p. 241.

salvation as there are citizens: Hobbes wants uniformity in the interest of stability. But his method again diminishes respect for the sacred books. He himself indulges in some daring historical criticism of the attributions of authorship of books of the Bible.[26]

Rather unexpectedly, though less so if we consider the social roots of his theories rather than the form those theories took, Hobbes approves of Independency so long as it does not degenerate into sectarian anarchy.[27] But that is really only a measure of his indifference, of his approval of the Independent separation of politics from theology, of the tendency of Independency to approach deism and rationalism. For though Hobbes is prepared through indifference to defend political intolerance, still tolerance at least of opinions not translated into actions —is more natural to him. "But what reason is there for it?" he asks of persecution. "Is it because such opinions are contrary to true Religion? that cannot be, if they be true. Let therefore the truth be first examined by competent Judges, or confuted by them that pretend to know the contrary."[28] Here Hobbes links up with the sceptical or deist aristocrats of the Restoration period, with the whole drift of political thought to the sort of practical toleration *de covenance* realized after 1688, in which considerations of expediency and the welfare of trade played a far greater rôle than the passion for liberty of a Milton. "Forasmuch as some ease to scrupulous consciences in the exercise of religion may be an effectual means to unite their Majesties' Protestant subjects in interest and affection . . ." ran the preamble to the Toleration Act of 1689, frankly. This is how Hobbes put it: "There is another Errour in their Civill Philosophy . . . to extend the power of the Law, which is the Rule of Actions onely, to the very Thoughts, and Consciences of men, by Examination, and *Inquisition* of what they hold, notwithstanding the Conformity of their Speech and Actions: By which, men are either punished for answering the truth of their thoughts, or constrained to answer an untruth for fear of punishment."[29] It is not the noblest strain in which to plead liberty of conscience, but it has proved perhaps the most acceptable political argument; and it is one for which the author of *Leviathan* has received insufficient credit.

[26] *Ibid.*, pp. 204–5.
[27] *Ibid.*, p. 380.
[28] *Ibid.*, p. 376.
[29] *Ibid.*, p. 374.

The scientific spirit of Hobbes is most clearly shown in the structure of *Leviathan* itself. . . .

Hobbes tries to reduce the rational process to calculation. "For REASON, in this sense, is nothing but *Reckoning* (that is, Adding and Subtracting) of the Consequences of generall names agreed upon, for the *marking* and *signifying* of our thoughts."[30] This is a kind of Benthamite calculus, borrowed from the counting-house and the merchant's ledger: as bourgeois as Benjamin Franklin.

Together with this goes a denial of all metaphysical absolutes. Hobbes's corroding scepticism worked a revolution of destruction in the world of thought parallel to that which was taking place in institutions and social standards. Hobbes has no use at all for conventional moral exhortations. "For one man calleth *Wisdome,* what another calleth *feare;* and one cruelty, what another *justice.* . . . And therefore such names can never be the true grounds of any ratiocination." Standards are entirely relative, except for Leviathan's arbitrary absolutes. "Whatsoever is the object of any mans Appetite or Desire; that is it, which he for his part calleth Good."[31] And this moves over to politics. "The doctrine of Right and Wrong, is perpetually disputed, both by the Pen and the Sword: Whereas the doctrine of Lines, and Figures, is not so; because men care not, in that subject, what be truth, as a thing that crosses no mans ambition, profit or lust. For I doubt not, but if it had been a thing contrary to any mans right of dominion, or to the interest of men that have dominion, *That the three Angles of a Triangle, should be equall to two Angles of a Square;* that doctrine should have been, if not disputed, yet by the burning of all books of Geometry, suppressed, as farre as he whom it concerned was able." The laws of nature, therefore, are precepts or general rules, found out by knowing the consequences, by book-keeping, by counting the cost.[32] A man would be irrational, unaware of his own best interests if he did not observe them, just as a merchant would be a fool if, having once learned to keep accounts, he let his affairs get into confusion by failing to keep them.

There are various hints which suggest that Hobbes would agree with Rousseau in holding that no true commonwealth, in his sense of the term, has ever yet existed: that he was legislating for the

[30] *Ibid.,* p. 18.
[31] *Ibid.,* pp. 18, 24.
[32] *Ibid.,* pp. 18, 52–3, 66.

future. In the chapter "Of Dominion Paternall, and Despoticall", he wrote: "The greatest objection is, that of the Practise; when men ask, where, and when, such Power has by Subjects been acknowledged. But one may ask them again, when or where has there been a Kingdome long free from Sedition and Civill Warre. . . . For though in all places of the world, men should lay the foundation of their houses on the sand, it could not thence be inferred, that so it ought to be." [33] "So, long time after men have begun to constitute Common-wealths, imperfect, and apt to relapse into disorder, there may, Principles of Reason be found out, by industrious meditation, to make their constitutions (excepting by externall violence) everlasting. And such are those which I have in this discourse set forth." [34]

Hobbes knows that a new world has come into existence, to which the standards of the old order will no longer apply. No revolutionary himself, all the assumptions of his approach to politics are new, radical, and "bourgeois"—though stripped of the religious swaddling clothes in which opposition thought was still clothed. Rousseau had only to insist that sovereignty must and could lie in the people alone, in order to convert Hobbes's political philosophy into a revolutionary creed that would overthrow the thrones of Europe.

[33] *Ibid.*, pp. 109–10; cf. p. 93. Clarendon takes this up, naturally enough: "He will introduce a Government of his own devising" (*A Brief View* . . . , pp. 46–7).

[34] *Leviathan*, p. 179.

PURITANISM AS A REVOLUTIONARY IDEOLOGY *

Michael Walzer

Michael Walzer teaches political theory at Princeton University. He has written several articles on the Puritans and his book about their political ideas is to be published soon.

It is obvious that Bunyan's pilgrim would hardly set out on his strange journey in such a stable bourgeois society as that of nineteenth-century England. Nor, since Christian is everyman and no medieval saint, would he set out from a stable feudal society. He "corresponds" to what can roughly be called a time of transition. But the time of transition, a time of instability and chronic danger, is only the *condition* of his journey–its cause is ideological. And it is the journey in its ideological setting, complete with purpose and meaning, which constitutes the experience and needs to be explained.

In order to get at the world of experience, it may well be necessary to construct some highly abstract model of economic processes and social change. But this construct is not "real life". It is only an intellectual approach to reality and only one among several possible approaches. The Marxist historian seeks to reconstitute the world which is perceived, while at the same time detaching himself from the particular perceptions of historical men. But it ought to be those very perceptions which direct his work. Reality is too complex, too detailed, too formless: he can never reproduce it. He must seek, instead, to reproduce only those aspects of historical existence which were, so to speak, absorbed into the experience of particular men. And if he is to avoid anachronistic reconstructions, his guide must be the men themselves. It would be absurd to assume *a priori* that what is of central importance

* Reprinted by permission of the author and of the editor of *History and Theory* from "Puritanism as a Revolutionary Ideology," *History and Theory*, III, 1961, pp. 75–90.

in late sixteenth- and early seventeenth-century history is, for example, the growth of the coal industry. One must look first to see what impact such a phenomenon had upon the lives of men. It is not, of course, only a question of whether they talked about it, but of whether they *felt* it, directly or indirectly, consciously or unconsciously. If they did not, then its significance must be sought in the future.

Marxists become the victims of the very alienation they claim to understand so well when they reverse this procedure and make experience dependent upon what is originally only a creation of the mind. When Tawney writes that Puritanism is the "magic mirror" in which the middle-class man saw himself ennobled and enhanced, he is in no sense enlightening us as to the historical process by which Puritanism developed and spread. For the Puritan is a real man, who can be encountered in history. But the middle-class man is made up, and it is sheer anachronism to describe him as a historical figure, articulate, already in search of an enhanced image. It has been suggested above that Puritanism is a part of the process (the long succession of perceptions and responses) by which men *become* middle-class. But to know the particular perceptions upon which it is based or the responses it prescribes, it is necessary to know the Puritan. There is, in fact, no magic mirror; sainthood is no mere enhancement of an already established (even if worrisome) identity. It is a far more active thing than that; it is indeed what Weber suggests—a way of forming an identity.

What must be studied, then, is a mind, or a group of minds, coping with problems and not passively reflecting them. For the mind mediates between the "objective" situation and the human act and if the act is to be understood, the mind must first be known. The problems it faces are posed by an environment which can of course be analyzed in some objective fashion—for example, statistically. But different aspects of this environment are experienced by different men with different results in consciousness and behavior. Hence the "objective" construct is of no independent value and has no prior significance in explanation. The first task of the historian is to establish his familiarity with the experience of particular men, with their difficulties, aspirations and achievements, and with the styles in which all these are expressed. This is not to suggest that the historical record should be taken at face value, or the assumption casually made that men always mean what they say. There is, for example, false piety and evasion among the saints which the historian must expose. There is caution and conformity which he must respect, but not too much. For hindsight is also insight into the concealments of respectability and of "Aesopian" prose; and it is often insight as well into purposes half-understood and patterns of thought not yet fully worked out. Hence the methods of the historian must be sceptical, devious and experimental, even while his general approach is open and sympathetic. But ultimately his sympathy is the key to all else: the best judgment of face value will be made by men with some intuitive understanding of other levels of thinking and feeling. . . .

If Puritanism is studied with these ideas in mind, a new light is thrown on sixteenth- and seventeenth-century history. One searches more deeply in the life experience of the saints for those feelings of fearfulness which parallel the belief in witches—and for the sources of such fear. One searches for sudden changes in environment, habits, authorities. The result is a hypothesis which is in striking contradiction to that of the Marxists: Puritanism appears to be a response to disorder and fear, a way of organizing men to overcome the acute sense of chaos. With this hypothesis it becomes possible to understand, for example, the as yet fragmentary evidence which suggests that the Calvinist faith, especially in its more radical forms, appealed most of all to men newly come to London and not, as Marxists have always assumed, to experienced city dwellers.[1] For coming to the city was an event in a man's life which might well sharpen his sense of danger and even lead him to seek that discipline which has been described above as central to Puritan association. Thus, the sudden increase in London's population between roughly 1580 and 1625 takes on new significance: it may well be that London did not so much prepare men to become "saints" as that sainthood helped them, through the hard transition period, to become Londoners. Once they had become *urbane,* they were in fact unlikely to remain faithful to the original Calvinist creed; they became revisionists. Similarly, it is somewhat less of a paradox than Marxists might suppose that witchcraft should range more widely in the southeast of England, where economic development was most advanced. For it may be—and this, perhaps, can be investigated—that witchcraft helped solve, in the minds of the people, some of the prob-

[1] On the growth of London, see the figures in F. P. Wilson, *The Plague in Shakespeare's London* (Oxford, 1927), appendix. That members of Puritan conventicles were often newcomers to the city is suggested by the court records reprinted in Champlin Burrage, *The Early English Dissenters in the Light of Recent Research 1550–1641* (Cambridge, 1912), II.

lems raised by that very development and by its impact upon traditional ways of doing things. (This is, of course, only speculation, but it is speculation which begins at the right place: with a concern for the concerns of the Puritans themselves.)

It seems likely that certain modes of perception and response parallel certain basic historical experiences; if so, comparison is possible and one might arrive at general propositions. But the relationship between, for example, urbanization and some ideological response to urbanization (once again, it must be said that these are not distinct "spheres") must be understood in dynamic terms. Perhaps it would be best to figure to oneself an energetic man continually struggling to understand and cope with the surrounding world. Undoubtedly, energy and struggle are not universal in history: ways of thinking quickly become habitual, as does experience itself. But it is the creative moments which require explanation and at such moments ideology is never a mere habit or reflex, but a willful activity. For perhaps a hundred years after the original creative achievement of Calvin, the spread of Puritanism can still be described in the active tense: men, with their own problems and aspirations, continually rediscovered for themselves, with all the enthusiasm which must have attended the first discovery, the truths of the new faith. The historian who begins with these ideology-producing men may then work outward, so to speak, re-experiencing their world and only after this subjecting that world to such further analysis as will improve his own understanding of it.

The Puritan saints are such men, making their ideology, and making themselves. The sources and nature of this creativity must next be considered.

The study of the Puritans is best begun with the idea of discipline, and all the tension and strain that underlies it, both in their writing and in what can be known of their experience. It is strange that theorists have had so little to say on this topic, especially since the rebellion against Puritan repression, or rather against its ugly remnants —devoid, as Weber's capitalism is, of theological reason—is still a part of our own experience. The persecution of witches, of course, was not a vital aspect of Puritan endeavor, but the active, fearful struggle against wickedness was. And the saints imagined wickedness as a creative and omnipresent demonic force, .that is, as a continuous threat. Like Hobbes, they saw disorder and war as the natural state of fallen men, out of which they had been drawn by God's command and by the painful efforts of their own regenerate wills. But they lived always on the very brink of chaos, maintaining their position only through a constant vigilance and, indeed, a constant warfare against their own natural inclinations and against the devil and his worldlings.

The goal of this warfare was repression and its apparent cause was an extraordinary anxiety. It is by no means necessary to argue that these two constitute the "essence" of Puritanism, only that their full significance has not been realized. In Calvin's own work anxiety is presented as central to the experience of fallen man: this is anxiety of a special sort; it is not the fear of death and damnation, but rather the fear of sudden and violent death. Hobbes would recognize it as the dominant passion of man in his natural state. Thus Calvin: [2]

> Now, whithersoever you turn, all the objects around you are not only unworthy of your confidence, but almost openly menace you, and seem to threaten immediate death. Embark in a ship; there is but a single step between you and death. Mount a horse; the slipping of one foot endangers your life. Walk through the streets of a city; you are liable to as many dangers as there are tiles on the roofs. If there be a sharp weapon in your hand, or that of your friend, the mischief is manifest. All the ferocious animals you see are armed for your destruction. If you endeavor to shut yourself in a garden surrounded with a good fence, and exhibiting nothing but what is delightful, even there sometimes lurks a serpent. Your house, perpetually liable to fire, menaces you by day with poverty, and by night with falling on your head. Your land, exposed to hail, frost, drought and various tempests, threatens you with sterility, and with its attendant, famine. I omit poison, treachery, robbery and open violence, which partly beset us at home and partly pursue us abroad . . . You will say that these things happen seldom, or certainly not always nor to every man, [and] never all at once. I grant it; but we are admonished by the examples of others, that it is possible for them to happen to us. . . .

Among the saints such terrible fearfulness was overcome, and that was the great benefit of sainthood: it did not so much promise future ecstasy as present "tranquillity". "When the light of Divine Providence," wrote Calvin, "has once shined on a pious man, he is relieved and delivered not only from the extreme anxiety and dread with which he was previously oppressed, but also from all care." [3] But relief was

[2] *Institutes of the Christian Religion* (Allen translation), Book, I, chapter XVII, x.

[3] *Ibid.*, xi.

not rest in the Calvinist world; it was rather that security of mind which might well manifest itself as self-righteousness—or as fanaticism.

In Puritan literature this same fearfulness is made specific in social terms. Once again, it is a fear which Hobbes would understand: the fear of disorder in society. It is apparent in the nervous hostility with which Puritan writers regarded carousal, vagabondage, idleness, all forms of individualistic extravagance (especially in clothing), country dances and urban crowds, the theater with its gay (undisciplined) audiences, gossip, witty talk, love-play, dawdling in taverns—the list could be extended.[4] The shrewdest among their contemporaries sensed that this pervasive hostility was a key to Puritanism—though they could hardly help but regard it as hypocritical. Ben Jonson's Zeal-of-the-land Busy is a caricature based, like all good caricatures, on a kernel of truth. Zeal-of-the-land is, for all his comical hypocrisy, insistently and anxiously concerned about the world he lives in—and the aim of his concern is supervision and repression.[5]

At times, Puritan preachers sounded very much like Hobbes: ". . . take sovereignty from the face of the earth," proclaimed Robert Bolton, "and you turn it into a cockpit. Men would become cut-throats and cannibals . . . Murder, adulteries, incests, rapes, robberies, perjuries, witchcrafts, blasphemies, all kinds of villainies, outrages and savage cruelty would overflow all countries." [6] But secular sovereignty was not their usual appeal. They looked rather to congregational discipline, as has been argued above. Thus Thomas Cartwright promised that the new discipline would restrain stealing, adultery and murder. Even more, it would "correct" sins "which the magistrate doth not commonly punish"—he listed lying, jesting, choleric speeches.[7] It need hardly be said that John Locke, a century later, was not terribly worried about such sins. Walsingham's spies reported in the 1580's and '90's that Puritan agitators were promising "that if discipline were planted, there should be no more vagabonds nor beggars". John Penry

[4] Alfred Harbage has pointed out that Puritans objected more to the audience at the theaters than to the plays: see his *Shakespeare's Audience* (New York, 1951).

[5] Jonson, *Bartholomew Fair;* see also his characterizations of two Puritans in *The Alchemist.*

[6] Bolton, *Two Sermons* (London, 1635), I, 10. The passage is a curious one since it opens with a paraphrase of Hooker, *Ecclesiastical Polity,* I, iii, 2; but Hooker says nothing about the effects of disobedience *among men,* which is the Puritan writer's chief concern.

[7] John Whitgift, *Works,* I, 21.

foresaw the "amendment" of idleness and hence, he thought, of poverty.[8] Now none of these concerns was unusual in Tudor or early Stuart England, but the intensity and extent of Puritan worry and the novelty of the proposed solution have no parallel among statesmen or traditional moralists. These latter groups also watched with apprehension the growth of London, the increasing geographic and social mobility, and the new forms of individualistic experimentation. It must be said, however, that the tone of their writings rarely reached a pitch of anxiety and fearfulness comparable to, for example, the diary of the Puritan minister Richard Rogers, endlessly worried about his own "unsettledness". Nostalgia was a more common theme, satire and mockery a more frequent defense among moralists like Thomas Dekker.[9] And the world they would have substituted for Renaissance England was an already romanticized version of medieval England. Not so the Puritans. Their discipline would have established dramatically new forms of association: the anxiety of the minister Rogers led him to join with his brethren in a solemn covenant—and these brethren were neither his immediate neighbors nor his kinfolk.[10]

What Rogers sought from his covenant was a bolstering of his faith, a steeling of his character. "The sixth of this month [December, 1587] we fasted betwixt ourselves," he reported in his diary, ". . . to the stirring up of ourselves to greater godliness." The need for this "stirring up" is so pervasive among the Puritans that one might well imagine that what they feared so greatly was rather in themselves than in the society about them. In fact, what they feared was the image in themselves of the "unsettledness" of their world. Puritan fearfulness is best explained in terms of the actual experiences of exile, alienation, and social mobility about which the saints so often and insistently wrote.[11] Discipline and repression are responses to these experiences, responses which do not aim at a return to some former security, but rather at a vigorous control and a narrowing of energies—a bold effort to shape a

[8] The report to Walsingham is quoted in Hill, *Puritanism and Revolution,* 234. John Penry, *An Humble Motion with Submission* (Edinburgh, 1590), 72.

[9] The views of the moralists are described in L. C. Knights, *Drama and Society in the Age of Jonson* (London, 1937).

[10] *Two Elizabethan Diaries,* ed. M. Knappen (Chicago, 1933), 69.

[11] They wrote about more than these themes, of course, and even here described more than their own experience, for the outsider is an archetypal figure realized with especial force in Christian thought. The Puritans still lived within a cultural tradition which shaped their expression as it undoubtedly still shaped their experience. On the dangers of reductionism, see Leavis, *op. cit.,* 208–10.

personality amidst "chaos". Thus might be explained the extraordinarily regimented life recorded in Margaret Hoby's diary. Mrs. Hoby was a merchant's daughter, married to a gentleman (the son of the Elizabethan ambassador Sir Thomas Hoby, translator of Castiglione) and carried off to a country estate in Yorkshire where all her neighbors were Catholic and, in her eyes, rowdy and sinful men. There she spent her time in earnest conversations with her minister, reading and listening to sermons and laboriously copying them out in her notebook, adhering to a strict routine of public and private prayer, assiduous in her daily self-recrimination: [12]

> I talked of some things not so as I ought when I had considered of them, but I find what is in a man if the Lord's spirit do never so little hide itself . . . but this is my comfort, that my heart is settled to be more watchful hereafter. . . .

How many men have settled since for the same "comfort"!

Undoubtedly, Margaret Hoby's behavior might be differently explained, but not so as to account so well for the similar behavior of her brethren. These people felt themselves exceptionally open to the dangers about them and this must have been, in part, because they were cut off, as were the men who succumbed to chaos—beggars and vagabonds—from the old forms of order and routine. It is this sense of being cut off, alien, that is expressed in the endless descriptions of the saint as a stranger and pilgrim which are so important in Puritan writing.[13] Pilgrimage is, perhaps, one of the major themes in all Christian literature, but it achieves among the Puritans a unique power, a forcefulness and intensity in its popular expression which culminates finally in Bunyan's classic. Over and over again, with the detail which only experience or, perhaps, a continually engaged imagination can give, Puritans describe life as a journey (or, in the image which Hobbes later made famous, as a race) through alien country. And yet, at the same time, they write of the vagabond with venomous hatred: he is a dangerous man because he has not disciplined and prepared himself for his journey. "Wandering beggars and rogues," wrote William Perkins, "that pass from place to place, being under no certain magistracy or ministry, nor joining themselves to any set society in

[12] *Diary of Lady Margaret Hoby, 1559–1605,* ed. D. M. Meads (London, 1930), 97.

[13] See the comments of William Haller on Puritan wayfaring: *The Rise of Puritanism* (New York, 1957), 147 ff.

church or commonwealth, are plagues and banes of both, and are to be taken as main enemies of [the] ordinance of God . . ." [14] The bitterness of this passage suggests the self-hatred of the Puritan pilgrim, pitying and worrying about his own "unsettledness". When the famous preacher Richard Greenham told a Puritan audience "Paradise is our native country", some of his listeners surely must have winced to think: *not England*. "We dwell here as in Meshech and as in the tents of Kedar, and therefore we be glad to be at home." It was painful, but inevitable, that the saints should live in tents. Perkins himself wrote in the same vein, for all his hatred of the wanderer: "Alas, poor souls, we are no better than passengers in this world, our way it is in the middle of the sea." [15] For many Puritans, if not for Perkins himself, who grew old in Cambridge, these words must have had a meaning both literal and poignant. Since the days of Mary, exile had been a common experience for the saints. And a generation after Perkins wrote, the "middle of the sea" would become a path for tens of thousands.

The fanatical self-righteousness of that first Puritan John Knox, a Scottish peasant's son, set loose in Europe by war and revolution, is surely in some sense a function of his exile: righteousness was a consolation and a way of organizing the self for survival. The "unsettledness" of Richard Rogers was due in part to his devious struggles with the corporate church and its bishops; but Rogers, who remembered his Essex birthplace as a "dunghill", was ever an outsider, and Puritanism his way of stirring up his heart. When William Whitgift, the future archbishop, cruelly taunted the Puritan leader Thomas Cartwright for "eating at other men's tables", he was perhaps suggesting an important source of Cartwright's vision of congregational unity and holiness. Margaret Hoby's life would have been different indeed had she been raised in a traditional country family: there would, for example, have been dancing at her wedding, and her life thereafter would hardly have allowed for time-consuming religious exercises. Deprived of such a life, because of her social background (and the ideas which were part of it) or, perhaps, because of basic changes in rural life, she willfully sought new comforts.[16] Country gentlemen like John Winthrop

[14] William Perkins, *Works* (London, 1616), III, 539; the passage is quoted in Hill, *op. cit.*, 228.

[15] Greenham, *Works* (London, 1605), 645; Perkins, *op. cit.*, I, 398.

[16] *Two Elizabethan Diaries*, 17; A. F. Scott-Pearson, *Thomas Cartwright and Elizabethan Puritanism* (Cambridge, 1925), 66; *Diary of Margaret Hoby*, 32—at their wedding, the Hobys sought "only to please the beholders with a sermon and a dinner."

and Oliver Cromwell, educated at Cambridge, knowledgeable in London, suddenly turned upon the traditional routine of English life as if it were actually vicious. Half in, half out of that routine, they anxiously sought a new certainty. "Oh, I lived in and loved darkness and hated light; I was a chief, the chief of sinners", wrote Cromwell of his seemingly ordinary and conventional life before conversion. But now, he went on, "my soul is with the congregation of the first born, my body rests in hope; and if here I may honor my God either by doing or by suffering, I shall be most glad." [17]

All this suggests once again the view of Puritanism as a response of particular men to particular experiences of confusion, change, alienation and exile. Now Calvinism obviously made men extremely sensitive to disorder in all its forms. It is more important, however, that it gave meaning to the experience of disorder and provided a way out, a return to certainty. It was an active response, and not a mere reflection of social confusion, for indeed other men responded differently. There is no rigid pattern in these responses. It seems probable that members of a rising middle class most sharply experienced that alienation from old England which drove men to the exercises of sainthood. On the other hand, there were both gentlemen and citizens who certainly enjoyed the new freedoms of mobility, extravagance, individuality and wit, and eagerly sought entrance to the Renaissance court, where freedom was cultivated. And from among these men undoubtedly came many future capitalists. It would not be easy to explain in particular cases why the court held such attractions for some men, while it was vicious and iniquitous in the eyes of others. No more is it readily comprehensible why some of the newcomers to the burgeoning city of London merged into the mob or explored the exciting underworld, while others hated the wickedness of the city and sought out virtuous brethren in the radical conventicles. What is important for the present is that Puritanism was a response to an experience which many men had; it provided one way of understanding the experience and of coping with it.

Coping with it meant being reborn as a new man, self-confident and free of worry, capable of vigorous, willful activity. The saints sometimes took new names to signify their rebirth. If alienation had made them anxious, depressed, unable to work, given to fantasies of demons,

[17] *Cromwell's Letters and Speeches*, ed. Carlyle (London, 1893), I, 79–80. On Winthrop see E. S. Morgan, *The Puritan Dilemma: The Story of John Winthrop* (Boston, 1958).

morbid introspection or fearful daydreams such as Calvin had suggested were common among fallen men, then sainthood was indeed a transformation.[18] Cromwell's pledge to honor his God "by doing" was no idle boast: he was obviously capable of just that. Perhaps this transformation gave businessmen the confidence necessary for innovation or freed them from the necessity of feeling guilty about routine connivance, usury, extortion. Thus argue Marxists and Weberians alike. But innovation was more likely due to the recklessness of the speculator than to the self-confidence of the saint; indeed, the saints hated the "projectors" who lived in and about the court, currying favor and waiting for opportunity. The congregational discipline, as has been seen, would have established controls hardly compatible with businesslike hard dealing. Cromwell's "doing" was obviously of a different order, and Cromwell was a representative man. His life suggests that the Puritan experience produced first of all a political activist.

The Puritan new man was active not so that success might reinforce his self-esteem, but in order to transform a world in which he saw his own ever-present wickedness writ large.[19] In a sense, his was a struggle to free himself from temptation by removing all alternatives to godliness, by organizing his own life as a continuous discipline and society as a regiment. His activity was political in that it was always concerned with government—though not only or, perhaps, not most importantly, at the level of the state. Puritans often imagined the congregation as a "little commonwealth", replacing the organic imagery of Anglicans and Catholics with expressions deliberately drawn from the world of coercion and sovereignty. Thus they made manifest their own pervasive concern with *control* rather than with harmony or love.[20] Their treat-

[18] Indeed, Calvin thought that commercial competition, with its attendant anxiety, was an aspect of the life of *fallen* man; he pictured him nervously murmuring to himself: "I must use such a mean, I must practise such a feat. I must look into such a business, or otherwise I shall be behindhand in all things. I shall but pine away, I shall not get half my living, if I proceed not in this manner . . .". *Sermons upon the Fifth Book of Moses* (London, 1583), 821. Presumably the saint would be free from such anxiety.

[19] Most of the calls for activity in Puritan sermons are put in terms of the struggle against social disorder; activity is rarely described as a way of overcoming the fear of damnation. The clear emphasis of the preachers is on the social effects of hard work, and not, as Weber thought, on success as a spiritual sign. See, for example, the discussion of work in Robert Cleaver and John Dod, *A Godly Form of Household Government* (London, 1621), Sig. P 6 and 7.

[20] See Walter Travers, *A Fall and Plain Declaration of Ecclesiastical Discipline out of the Word of God* (n. p., 1574).

ment of the family was similar: they saw it as a field for the exercise of discipline by a godly father usually described as a "governor". Puritan interest in the family parallels that of Jean Bodin (though, in contrast to Robert Filmer, also a Bodinian, the saints had little to say about paternal affection and benevolence) and probably has the same source. The insistence upon the absolute sovereignty of the father and upon the family as an institution for repressing and disciplining naturally wicked, licentious and rebellious children derives in both cases from an extraordinary fear of disorder and anarchy. Thus two Puritan preachers in a famous treatise on "family government":

> The young child which lieth in the cradle [is] both wayward and full of affections: and though his body be but small, yet he hath a great heart, and is altogether inclined to evil. . . . If this sparkle be suffered to increase, it will rage over and burn down the whole house. For we are changed and become good, not by birth, but by education. . . . Therefore parents must be wary and circumspect, that they never smile or laugh at any words or deeds of their children done lewdly . . . naughtily, wantonly . . . they must correct and sharply reprove their children for saying or doing ill. . . .[21]

The father was continually active, warily watching his children; the elders of the congregation were ever alert and vigilant, seeking out the devious paths of sin; so also the godly magistrate. "In you it is now to cleanse, to free your country of villainy," a Puritan minister told the judges of Norwich, ". . . consider your power to reform . . . if you be faithful, and God's power to revenge if you be faithless."[22] In Puritan writings, political activity was described as a form of work: it required systematic application, attention to detail, sustained interest and labor. Much that the godly magistrates undertook might be called, in Marxist terms, progressive; some of their activity, however, would clearly impede free economic activity. But description in these terms is valuable only if one seeks to understand those aspects of Puritan activity which, through a subsequent process of selection, became permanent features of the modern world. In the seventeenth century, Puritan politics obviously had an interest rather different from that suggested by the term "progress". Its immediate purpose was to regain control of a changing world; hence the great concern with method, discipline, and order, and the frequent uneasiness with novelty. When the saints spoke of reform, they meant first of all an overcoming of social instability and

[21] Cleaver and Dod, *op. cit.*, Sig. S 8; Bodin, *op. cit.*, 9-13.
[22] Thomas Reed, *Moses Old Square for Judges* (London, 1632), 98–99.

all its moral and intellectual concomitants. Godly magistracy was a bold effort to seize control of society, much as sainthood had been an effort to control and organize the self. And the first of these followed from the second: in this way did Puritanism produce revolutionaries. In much the same way, it may be suggested, did the Jacobin man of virtue become an *active citizen,* and the hardened and "steeled" Bolshevik first a *professional* revolutionary and then, in Lenin's words, a "leader", "manager", and "controller".[23]

These revolutionary men do not simply attack and transform the old order—as in the Marxist story. The old order is only a part, and often not the most important part, of their experience. They live much of their lives amidst the breakdown of that order, or in hiding or exile from it. And much of their rebellion is directed against the very "unsettledness" that they know best. The analogy with the Bolsheviks is worth pursuing. Lenin's diatribes against "slovenliness . . . carelessness, untidiness, unpunctuality, nervous haste, the inclination to substitute discussion for action, talk for work, the inclination to undertake everything under the sun without finishing anything" were intended first of all as attacks upon his fellow exiles—whatever their value as descriptions of the "primitive" Russia he hated so much.[24] The first triumph of Bolshevism, as of Puritanism, was over the impulse toward "disorganization" in its own midst: here, so to speak, was Satan at work where he is ever most active—in the ranks of the godly. And it must be said that this triumph was also over the first impulses toward freedom. Thus the Puritans vigorously attacked Renaissance experimentation in dress and in all the arts of self-decoration and hated the free-wheeling vagabonds who "crowd into cities [and] boroughs . . . roll up and down from one lodging to another", never organizing themselves into families and congregations.[25] Similarly, the Jacobin leader Robespierre attacked the economic egotism of the new bourgeoisie and spitefully connected the radical free thought of the Enlightenment with anti-revolutionary conspiracy. Atheism, he declared, is aristocratic.[26]

[23] Lenin, *The Immediate Tasks of the Soviet Government* (1918) in *Selected Works* (New York, 1935–1937), VII, 332–33.

[24] *How To Organize Competition* (1917, reprinted Moscow, 1951), 63; also see *Letters* trans. and ed. by Elizabeth Hill and Doris Mudie (New York, 1937), 161.

[25] Henry Crosse, *Virtue's Commonwealth* (London, 1603), Sig. L_4 *vers;* Perkins, *Works,* III, 191.

[26] Quoted in A. Aulard, *Christianity and the French Revolution* (Boston, 1927), 113.

And again Lenin, preaching with all the energy of a secular Calvinist against free love: "Dissoluteness in sexual life is bourgeois, [it] is a phenomenon of decay. The proletariat is a rising class . . . It needs clarity, clarity and again clarity. And so, I repeat, no weakening, no waste, no destruction of forces." [27]

In fact, Lenin's morality had little to do with the proletariat, and the "dissoluteness" he attacked had little to do with the bourgeoisie. He might as well have talked of saints and worldlings as the Puritans did. The contrast he was getting at was between those men who had succumbed to (or taken advantage of!) the disorder of their time—speculators in philosophy, vagabonds in their sexual life, economic Don Juans—and those men who had somehow pulled themselves out of "unsettledness", organized their lives and regained control. The first group were the damned and the second the saved. The difference between them was not social but ideological.

Puritans, Jacobins and Bolsheviks did tend to come from the same social strata—that is, from the educated middle classes, preachers, lawyers, journalists, teachers, professional men of all sorts. But this is not because such men are representatives of larger social groups whose interests they defend. It has already been shown that the connection between Puritan theory and bourgeois interests is at best a difficult one, which is in no sense implicit in the theory, but is rather worked out later in a long process of corruption, selection and forgetting. Men like the godly ministers speak first of all for themselves: they record most sensitively the experience of "unsettledness" and respond to it most vigorously. For reasons which require further investigation, such men seem less integrated into their society—even in the most stable periods—and more available, as it were, for alienation than are farmers or businessmen. This is not, of course, to reduce their moral discipline (or their radical politics) to the psychological therapy of alienated intellectuals. The alienation which John Knox or Richard Rogers experienced, with all its attendant fearfulness and enthusiasm, sometimes

[27] Quoted in Klara Zetkin, "Reminiscences of Lenin", in *The Family in the U.S.S.R.*, ed. Rudolf Schlesinger (London, 1949), 78. It should be said that in all the revolutions discussed above, there were men who did not follow the Puritan saints or the vanguard Bolsheviks in their attacks upon human freedom. These men, radical sectarians, secularists, anarchists, libertarians of many sorts, were the products of the same society and the same experience which produced the others. They rarely made good revolutionaries, however, precisely because they never felt the intense need to yield to an organization and a discipline.

disfiguring and sometimes ennobling, was only a heightened form of the feelings of other men—in a sense, of all men, for ultimately the sociological range of the Puritan response was very wide.

But the historian must also record that "unsettledness" was not a permanent condition and that sainthood was only a temporary role. For men always seek and find not some tense and demanding discipline, but some new routine. The saints failed in their effort to establish a holy commonwealth and, in one way or another, their more recent counterparts have also failed. What this suggests is not that the holy commonwealth was an impractical dream, the program of muddled, unrealistic men. In fact, Puritan ministers and elders (and fathers!) had considerable political experience and the holy commonwealth was in a sense achieved, at least among those men who most needed holiness. Nor is it correct to argue from the failure of the saints that Puritanism in its revolutionary form represents only a temporary triumph of "ideas" over "interest", a momentary burst of enthusiasm.[28] For such moments have their histories, and what needs to be explained is why groups of men, over a fairly long span of time, acquired such an intense interest in ideas like predestination and holiness. Puritan ideology was a response to real experience, therefore a practical effort to cope with personal and social problems. The inability of the saints to establish and maintain their holy commonwealth suggests only that these problems were limited in time to the period of breakdown and psychic and political reconstruction. When men stopped being afraid, or became less afraid, then Puritanism was suddenly irrelevant. Particular elements in the Puritan system were transformed to fit the new routine —and other elements were forgotten. And only then did the saint become a man of "good behavior", cautious, respectable, calm, ready to participate in a Lockeian society.

The argument of the preceding section may now be concluded: Puritanism was not a revolutionary ideology in the Marxist sense, reflecting the interests of a rising class. Such interests are in the seventeenth century better represented by parliamentarians and common lawyers who had their own ideology. The faith of the saints was rather a pe-

[28] This is the view of revolutionary enthusiasm suggested in Crane Brinton's book on the French Revolution, *Decade of Revolution* (New York, 1934) and again in his *Anatomy of Revolution* (New York, 1938). The analogy with religion argued in both books is, however, a very suggestive one.

culiarly intense response to the experience of social change itself, an experience which, in one way or another, set groups of men outside the established order. It should be obvious that this may be the result of either "rising" or "falling" in economic terms; mobility itself is the key, especially if the old social order is traditionalist, dependent for its stability upon popular passivity. The Puritan response produced revolutionaries, that is, saints, godly magistrates, men already disciplined (before the revolution begins) for the strenuous work of transforming all society and all men in the image of their own salvation. Such men, narrow, fanatical, enthusiastic, committed to their "work", have little to contribute to the development of either liberalism or capitalism. To expect freedom from their hands is to invite disappointment. Their great achievement is what is known in the sociology of revolution as the *terror,* the effort to create a holy commonwealth and to force men to be godly.

The contribution of these men to the future is the destruction of the old order. Alienated from its conventions and routines—from its comforts—they feel no nostalgia as they watch its slow decay. They are capable not only of establishing, underground, an alternative system, but also of making a frontal assault upon the old order itself, in the case of the Puritans, upon hierarchy and patriarchy, the central principles of traditional government. Their extraordinary self-confidence, won at some cost, as has been seen, makes them capable finally of killing the king. Here Weber's analysis is undoubtedly closer to the truth than that of the Marxists: the saints are entrepreneurs indeed, but in politics rather than in economics. They ruthlessly (and anxiously) pursue not wealth or even individual power—never rely on great men, warned a Puritan preacher—but *collective control* of themselves, of each other, of all England.

The Puritan struggle for collective control is not unique in history. The illustrations already drawn from Jacobin and Bolshevik experience suggest at least the possibility of a comparative study of revolutionary ideology. To "set up" such a comparison has been one of the purposes of the foregoing argument. It remains only to defend its usefulness: it is useful primarily, of course, because the encounter with sainthood is a part of our own experience.

On the level of ideology, of perception and response, comparisons of the Calvinist elect with the Jacobin men of virtue and the Bolshevik vanguard would not provide any test of the hypothetical description of

Puritanism as a response to breakdown, disorder, and social change. They would demonstrate only that the hypothesis can be extended to cover other cases: other men have also lived through the experience of exile and alienation and have shaped their characters in opposition to their environment. Other men have won a self-assurance akin to that of the saints, and it has permitted them similar forms of activity—radical, ruthless, experimental. This extension of the range of analysis is useful even if it does not permit scientific testing of the hypothesis. Comparison always brings new insight: the additional examples often require elaboration and correction of the original hypothesis, and at the same time the discovery of significant differences in similar cases defines its limits. Working back and forth between, say, Puritans and Bolsheviks may also avoid some of the dangers of anachronistic judgment which are probably inherent in a commitment to a single progress—to English history, for example, with its solemn advance from precedent to precedent. For if the foregoing argument is at all correct, then the saints are likely to be similar not to the men who came before or after them in English history, but to other men in other countries who lived through a similar time and shared some of the same experiences.

The conditions of these experiences obviously may be compared in a more systematic fashion. Measurements of social mobility of various sorts and careful studies of economic change both might be useful here, though it must be said again that recording such measurements or carrying out such studies does not bring one face to face with "real life". Mobility, for example, is a different experience for different men. Nevertheless, it can surely be argued that urbanization under more or less similar conditions—which can be investigated and the details quarrelled over—makes a limited number of ideological responses likely, the appearance of a limited variety of new men probable. All these men may not be present in every case, but on a broad enough national scale and over a sufficient span of time, they are all likely to appear: the lost worldling whom the Puritans called damned, the exciting (and often creative) speculator in freedom, the fearful man who desperately seeks authority, and the saint himself.

But it is probably not possible in any particular place, at any moment in time, to predict the appearance of the last of these men—though it can be suggested, on the basis of the argument outlined above, that he will not be absent in a time of full-scale revolution. The ideas which shape his character are not automatic products of some objective development—indeed, very little is yet known about their production —and it is not easy to guess when they will take hold or what their precise nature will be. And here comparative work can only serve to increase the sensitivity of the student. If a science is not possible, then one must resort to an older form of knowledge, to that intuition which comes, above all, from the practice of history.

THE SOCIAL BEARINGS OF LOCKE'S POLITICAL THEORY *

C. B. Macpherson

C. B. Macpherson is professor of political science at the University of Toronto. He has written several essays in criticism of modern liberalism, as well as a book on English political theory from Hobbes to Locke, The Political Theory of Possessive Individualism *(Oxford: Oxford University Press, 1962).*

Locke did not make all his social assumptions explicit. There is no reason why he should have done so. The assumptions which he and his contemporary readers absorbed from the thinking of their own time, and from their understanding of their own society, he could take for granted.

Here I want to direct attention to two preconceptions which Locke, in common with many others of his class and time, entertained about his own society. As assumptions about the nature of seventeenth century society they are explicit in various writings of Locke; as assumptions about society in general they are implicit in the *Treatise* and had a decisive influence in his political theory.

These are (1) that while the laboring class is a necessary part of the nation, its members are not in fact full members of the body politic and have no claim to be so; and (2) that the members of the laboring class do not and cannot live a fully rational life. "Laboring class" is

* Reprinted by permission of the editor of *The Western Political Quarterly* from "The Social Bearings of Locke's Political Theory," *The Western Political Quarterly*, VII, 1954, pp. 4, 6–19.

used here to include both the "laboring poor" and the "idle poor," that is, all who were dependent on employment or charity or the workhouse because they had no property of their own by which, or on which, they might work.

That these people were not, in fact or by right, full members of political society was the prevailing view in England in the second half of the seventeenth century. They were regarded not as citizens but as a body of actual and potential labor available for the purposes of the nation. Professor Tawney has summarized their position in the observation that the prevailing attitude of English writers after 1660 "towards the new industrial proletariat [was] noticeably harsher than that general in the first half of the seventeenth century, and . . . has no modern parallel except in the behaviour of the less reputable of white colonists towards coloured labour." The working class was, in effect, in but not of civil society. . . .

Evidence of these assumptions is scattered throughout Locke's writings. His proposals for the treatment of the able-bodied unemployed are fairly well known, although when they are mentioned by modern writers it is usually to deprecate their severity and excuse it by reference to the standards of the time. What is more to the point is the view which these proposals afford of Locke's assumptions. Masters of workhouses ("houses of correction") were to be encouraged to make them into sweated-labor manufacturing establishments; justices of the peace were to make them into forced-labor institutions. Children of the unemployed "above the age of three" were unnecessarily a burden on the nation; they should be set to work, and could be made to earn more than their keep. All this was justified on the explicit ground that unemployment was due not to economic causes but to moral depravity. The multiplying of the unemployed, Locke wrote in 1697 in his capacity as a member of the Commission on Trade, was caused by "nothing else but the relaxation of discipline and corruption of manners." [1] There was no question in his mind of treating the unemployed as full or free members of the political community; there was equally no doubt that they were fully subject to the state. The state was entitled to deal with them in this way because they would not live up to the moral standard required of rational men.

[1] Quoted in H. R. Fox Bourne, *The Life of John Locke* (London, 1876), II, 378. Locke seems to have regarded the idle poor as depraved by choice, in contrast to the laboring poor, whom he considered incapable of a fully rational life because of their position.

Locke's attitude towards the employed wage-earning class has been noticed less often, though it is plain enough in various passages of his economic writings, particularly in *Some Considerations of the Consequences of the Lowering of Interest and Raising the Value of Money* (1691). There, incidentally to his technical arguments, Locke takes for granted that the wage-laborer constitutes a normal and sizable class in the nation,[2] that he has no property but is entirely dependent on his wages, and that, of necessity, his wages are normally at a bare subsistence level.[3] Such a person "just lives from hand to mouth." One passage in particular deserves quotation:

> . . . The labourer's share [of the national income], being seldom more than a bare subsistence, never allows that body of men, time, or opportunity to raise their thoughts above that, or struggle with the richer for theirs (as one common interest), unless when some common and great distress, uniting them in one universal ferment, makes them forget respect, and emboldens them to carve to their wants with armed force: and then sometimes they break in upon the rich, and sweep all like a deluge. But this rarely happens but in the maladministration of neglected, or mismanaged government.[4]

It is hard to say which part of these remarks is the most revealing. There is the assumption that the laborers are normally kept too low to be able to think or act politically. There is the assertion that maladministration consists not of leaving them there, but of allowing such unusual distress to occur as will unite them in armed revolt. And there is the conviction that such revolt is improper, an offense against the respect they owe to their betters.

Now the question: Who has the right of revolution? is a decisive question with Locke. The revolutionary right is to him the only effective test of citizenship, as he makes no provision for any other method of overthrowing an unwanted government. Although he insists, in the *Treatise,* on the majority's right to revolution, it does not seem to cross his mind here that the laboring class might have the right to make a revolution. Indeed there is no reason why such a thought should have occurred to him, for to him the laboring class was an object of state policy and of administration, rather than fully a part of the citizen

[2] *Considerations,* in *Works* (1759 edition), II, 13–16.
[3] *Ibid.,* p. 29.
[4] *Ibid.,* p. 36.

body. Such a class was incapable of rational political action, but the right to revolution depended essentially on rational decision.

The assumption that members of the laboring class are in too low a position to be capable of a rational life—that is, capable of regulating their lives by those moral principles Locke supposed were given by reason—is evident again in *The Reasonableness of Christianity*. The whole argument of that work is a plea that Christianity be restored to a few simple articles of belief "that the labouring and illiterate man may comprehend." Christianity should thus again be made

a religion suited to vulgar capacities; and the state of mankind in this world, destined to labour and travel. . . . The greatest part of mankind have not leisure for learning and logick, and superfine distinctions of the schools. Where the hand is used to the plough and the spade, the head is seldom elevated to sublime notions, or exercised in mysterious reasoning. 'Tis well if men of that rank (to say nothing of the other sex) can comprehend plain propositions, and a short reasoning about things familiar to their minds, and nearly allied to their daily experience. Go beyond this, and you amaze the greatest part of mankind. . . .[5]

This is not, as might be thought, a plea for a simple rationalist ethical religion to replace the disputations of the theologians. On the contrary, Locke's point is that without supernatural sanctions the laboring class is incapable of following a rationalist ethic. He only wants the sanctions made clearer. The simple articles he recommends are not moral rules, but articles of faith. Belief in them is all that is necessary, for such belief converts the moral rules of the gospel into binding commands. Locke's problem is to frame the articles so that they will appeal directly to the experience of the common people, who can thus believe. The greatest part of mankind, he concludes, cannot be left to the guidance of the laws of nature or of reason; they are not capable of drawing rules of conduct from them. For "the day-labourers and tradesmen, the spinsters and dairy maids . . . hearing plain commands, is the sure and only course to bring them to obedience and practice. The greatest part cannot know and therefore they must believe.". . .[6]

It would be surprising if Locke's preconceptions about his own society did not somehow affect his premises about society and man as

[5] *The Reasonableness of Christianity*, last two pages; *Works* (1759), II, 585–86.

[6] *Ibid.*, II, 580.

such. His unhistorical habit of mind presented no obstacle to his transferring assumptions about seventeenth-century society into a supposed state of nature. As he took his assumptions about his own society so much for granted that he felt no need to argue them, they could easily be carried into his premises without any consciousness of a problem of consistency. I shall argue that both of the assumptions about his own society—that of a class differential in rationality, and that of a class differential in rights—were generalized in Locke's thinking into implicit assumptions about human nature as such and about individual *natural* rights, and that these assumptions modified his explicit postulates about human nature and natural rights.

In Locke's initial statement of his postulates in the *Treatise* (and in his analysis of human nature in the *Essay Concerning Human Understanding,* which has to be considered also for a full statement of his general theory of human nature), there is nothing to suggest an assumption of class differentiation. However, before he used these postulates to deduce the necessary character of civil society, he put forward other arguments, especially in his treatment of property rights, which imply that he had already generalized his differential assumptions about his own society into abstract implicit assumptions of differential human nature and natural rights.

(1) Differential Rights. Locke found in seventeenth-century society a class differentiation so deep that the members of the laboring class had very different effective rights from the classes above them. They lived, and must live, "from hand to mouth," could never "raise their thoughts above that," and were unfit to participate in political life. Their condition was a result of their having no property on which they could expend their labor; their having no property was one aspect of the prevailing inequality which was grounded in "the necessity of affairs, and the constitution of human society." [7]

What Locke saw in his own society he considered typical of all civil society. But how did this become an assumption of differential *natural* rights, and where does it, as such an assumption, enter into the argument of the *Treatise?* It is certainly not present in the opening statements about natural rights; there the emphasis is all on the natural equality of rights (§§ 4, 5).[8]

[7] *Considerations, Works* (1759), II, 19.

[8] This and subsequent references in the text are to the section numbers of the *Second Treatise of Civil Government.* Quotations are from the 1764 edition of the *Treatises.*

The transformation of equal into differential natural rights comes to light in Locke's theory of property. In the chapter on property in the *Treatise,* he went out of his way to transform the natural right of every individual to such property as he needed for subsistence and to which he applied his labor, into a natural right of *unlimited* appropriation, by which the more industrious could rightfully acquire all the land, leaving others with no way to live except by selling the disposal of their labor.[9]

This transformation is not an aberration in Locke's individualism but an essential part of it. The core of his individualism is the assertion that every man is naturally the sole proprietor of his own person and capacities (§§ 4, 6, 44, 123)—the absolute proprietor in the sense that he owes nothing to society for them—and especially the absolute proprietor of his capacity to labor (§ 27). Every man is therefore free to alienate his own capacity to labor. This individualist postulate is the one by which Locke transforms the mass of equal individuals (rightfully) into two classes with very different rights, those with property and those without. Once the land is all taken up, the fundamental right not to be subject to the jurisdiction of another is so unequal between owners and nonowners that it is different in kind, not in degree: those without property are dependent for their livelihood on those with property and are unable to alter their own circumstances. The initial equality of natural rights, which consisted in no man's having jurisdiction over another (§ 4) cannot last after the differentiation of property. In other words, the man without property in things loses that proprietorship of his own person which was the basis of his equal natural rights. Locke insists that disparity in property is *natural,* that is, that it takes place "out of the bounds of society, and without compact" (§ 50). Civil society is established to protect unequal possessions, which have already in the natural state caused unequal rights. In this way Locke has generalized the assumption of a class differential in rights in his own society into an implicit assumption of differential *natural* rights. This implicit assumption, as will be seen, did not replace the initial theory of equality: both were in Locke's mind at the same time.

(2) Differential Rationality. We have seen that Locke assumed in his own society a class differential in rationality which left the laboring class incapable of a fully rational life. The questions are: How did this become an assumption of differential rationality in general? And

[9] "Locke on Capitalist Appropriation," *Western Political Quarterly,* IV, 550–66.

where did this enter the argument of the *Treatise?* It is clearly not present in the opening statements of postulates. There, rationality and depravity are dealt with abstractly and although rational men are distinguished from depraved men, there is no suggestion that the distinction is correlated with social class. But as the argument proceeds and the postulates have to be made more specific, it becomes apparent that Locke has something else in mind. When he has to relate depravity and rationality to man's political needs, these qualities turn out to have meaning only in the setting of a particular kind of property institutions and to be closely related to ownership.

Whatever man's inherent depravity may be, Locke thinks it does not require any but the most rudimentary political society until there is extensive property. Where there was "the equality of a simple poor way of living, confining [men's] desires within the narrow bounds of each man's small property," there would be few controversies and few trespasses, and consequently no need of many laws or magistrates; there would be more fear of outsiders than of each other, and the main purpose of setting up government would be for security "against foreign force" (§ 107). A fully civil society of the kind which is the main concern of the *Treatise,* a society for the internal security of individual property, is required for the protection not of small equal properties but only of extensive unequal ones, not of a modest store of consumables or perhaps a few acres of land but of a substantial accumulation of resources. It is the propensity to accumulate property beyond the requirements of subsistence that necessarily leads rational men to establish civil society.

Here we reach the crux of the matter. The propensity to accumulate, although it leads to quarrels, is itself not depraved but rational. Not only is the desire for accumulation rational, according to Locke, but accumulation is the essence of rational conduct. More precisely, the true nature of rational behavior is to expend labor improving the gifts of nature for subsequent enjoyment of greater real income or of greater power or prestige. This procedure, in Locke's view, requires private possession; and the measure of rational industriousness is the accumulation of possessions.

All this can be seen in the famous chapter on property in the *Treatise,* the burden of which is that the truly rational man is the industrious man. Rational behavior in temporal affairs is investing one's energies in the accumulation of real property and capital. "God gave the world to men in common; but . . . he gave it them . . . for . . . the greatest conveniences of life they were capable to draw from it. . . ." Therefore, He "gave it to the use of the industrious and rational," who would "improve" it (§ 34). Improvement without ownership is impossible: "The condition of human life, which requires labour and materials to work on, necessarily introduces private possessions" (§ 35). Not everyone in the state of nature could acquire property, for wherever money is introduced—and it is introduced in the state of nature (§ 50)—the land is all appropriated (§ 45). That the appropriation leaves some men without any possibility of getting land does not disturb Locke because the day-laborer in a society where the land is all appropriated is better off than the greatest man in a primitive economy (§ 41).

Thus "the industrious and rational" are not all laborers, but only those who acquire property and improve it by their labor.[10] A further effect of the introduction of money is that the rational goal of a man's industry becomes accumulation beyond any requirements of consumption. "Different degrees of industry" give men different amounts of property, and the invention of money gives the more industrious man the opportunity "to enlarge his possessions beyond the use of his family, and a plentiful supply to its consumption" (§ 48). In short, rational conduct, in the state of nature, consists in unlimited accumulation, the possibility of which is open only to some. It follows that there was, in Locke's view, a class differential in rationality in the state of nature, inasmuch as those who were left without property after the land was all appropriated could not be accounted fully rational. They had no opportunity to be so. Like day laborers in civil society they were not in a position to expend their labor improving the gifts of nature; their whole energies were needed to keep alive. They could not "raise their thoughts above that," for they just lived "from hand to mouth." . . .

The general theory presented at the opening of the *Treatise* affirms that men are naturally able to govern themselves by the law of nature, or reason. The state of nature, we are told, has a law of nature to govern it, which is reason (§ 6). The state of nature is contrasted flatly to the state of war: the two are "as far distant, as a state of peace, goodwill, mutual assistance and preservation, and a state of enmity, malice,

[10] The same conclusion is reached, from a different starting point, by Leo Strauss, in a penetrating recent article on natural law: "On Locke's Doctrine of Natural Rights," *Philosophical Review,* XLI (October, 1952), 495–96.

violence and mutual destruction, are from one another. Men living together according to reason, without a common superior on earth, with authority to judge between them, is properly the state of nature" (§ 19). It is no derogation of this view of the state of nature to allow, as Locke does, that there are some men in it who will not follow the law of nature. Nature's law teaches only those who will consult it (§ 6); some men transgress it and, by so doing, declare themselves "to live by another rule than that of reason and common equity" and in this way become "dangerous to mankind" (§ 8); a man who violates the law of nature "becomes degenerate, and declares himself to quit the principles of human nature, and to be a noxious creature" (§ 10). The whole picture of the state of nature in chapter ii of the *Treatise* is one of a people abiding by natural law, with some natural criminals among them: Locke even uses the word criminal to describe the man in the state of nature who violates its law (§ 8).

But this representation is only one of two quite opposite pictures Locke has of the state of nature. As early as chapter iii of the *Treatise,* only a page after the distinction between the state of nature and the state of war, we read that where there is no authority to decide between contenders "every the least difference is apt to end" in the "state of war," and that "one great reason of men's putting themselves into society, and quitting the state of nature" is "to avoid this state of war" (§ 21). The difference between the state of nature and the Hobbesian state of war has virtually disappeared. Some chapters later, we read further that the state of nature is "very unsafe, very unsecure"; that in it the enjoyment of individual rights is "very uncertain, and constantly exposed to the invasion of others," and that it is "full of fears and continual dangers." All this danger occurs because "the greater part [are] no strict observers of equity and justice" (§ 123). What makes the state of nature unlivable, according to this account, is not the viciousness of the few but the disposition of "the greater part" to depart from the law of reason.

The contradiction between Locke's two sets of statements about natural man is obvious. It is a central contradiction in the explicit postulates on which his political theory is built. It will not do to say he simply echoes the traditional Christian conception of man as a contradictory mixture of appetite and reason. Locke no doubt accepted that view; and within it there is room for a considerable variety of belief as to the relative weights (or potentialities) of the two ingredients of human nature. Different exponents of Christian doctrine could take different views. What has to be explained is how Locke took not one position in this matter but two opposite positions. . . .

It seems reasonable to conclude that Locke was able to take both positions about human nature because he had in mind simultaneously two conceptions of society, which, although logically conflicting, were derived from the same ultimate source. One was the seventeenth-century atomistic conception of society as a mass of equal, undifferentiated beings. The other was the notion of a society composed of two classes differentiated by their level of rationality—those who were "industrious and rational" and had property, and those who were not, who labored, indeed, but only to live, not to accumulate.

Locke was unconscious of the contradiction between these two conceptions of society because both of them (and not merely, as we have already seen, the second one) were elements transferred to his postulates from his comprehension of his own society. Ultimately it was Locke's comprehension of his own society that was ambiguous and contradictory. It could not have been otherwise, for it was the comprehension of an emerging bourgeois society, reflecting the ambivalence of a society which demanded formal equality but required substantive inequality of rights.

As a bourgeois philosopher, a proponent of seventeenth-century individualism, Locke had to regard men as equal, undifferentiated units, and to consider them rational. The bourgeois order justified itself by assuming, first, that all men were intellectually capable of shifting for themselves, and secondly, that rational behavior in this sense was morally rational, in accordance with the law of nature. Thus a necessary part of the bourgeois vision pictured man in general in the image of rational bourgeois man. Locke shared this view, which gave him the account of the state of nature as rational and peaceable.

At the same time, as a bourgeois philosopher Locke necessarily conceived abstract society as consisting of two classes with different rationality. The two classes in Locke's England lived lives totally different in freedom and rights. The basic difference between them in fact was the difference in their ability to live by the bourgeois moral code. But to the directing class this appeared to be a differential capacity in men to live by moral rules as such. This conception of society gave Locke the picture of the state of nature as unsafe and insecure. For to say, as he did, that most men are incapable of guiding their lives by the law of reason, without sanctions, is to say that a civil society with legal sanctions (and a church with spiritual sanctions) is needed to keep them in order. Without these sanctions, i.e., in a state of nature, there could be no peace.

Both views of the state of nature flowed from the bourgeois concept of society, and both were necessary to it. Their common source obscured their contradictory quality. There was no question of Locke's basing his theory on an Aristotelian concept of two classes—masters and slaves—whose relative positions were justified by a supposed inherent difference in rationality. With Locke the difference in rationality was not inherent in men; it was socially acquired by virtue of different economic positions. But since it was acquired in the state of nature, it was inherent in society. Once acquired, that is to say, it was permanent, for it was the concomitant of an order of property relations which Locke assumed to be the permanent basis of civilized society. His notion of differential rationality justified as natural, not slavery,[11] but the subordination of one part of the people by their continual contractual alienation of their capacity to labor. In the bourgeois view men were free to alienate their freedom, and Locke, at least, thought that the difference in rationality was a result rather than a cause of that alienation. But the difference in rationality, once established, provided a justification for differential rights.

The Ambiguous Civil Society

We may now inquire how Locke's ambiguous position on natural rights and rationality enters and affects his theory of the formation of civil society. Men enter into civil society, Locke asserts, to protect themselves from the inconveniences, insecurity and violence of the state of nature. Or, as he declares repeatedly, the great reason for men's uniting into society and putting themselves under government is to preserve their property, by which, he says, he means their "lives, liberties and estates" (§ 123, cf. § 173). When property is so defined, everyone has a reason to enter civil society, and everyone is capable of entering it, having some rights which he can transfer. However, Locke did not

[11] Locke did, of course, justify slavery also, but not on grounds of inherently differential rationality. Enslavement was justified only when a man had "by his fault forfeited his own life, by some act that deserves death" (§ 23). Locke appears to have thought of it as a fit penalty for his natural criminals.

keep to this definition. He used the term in two different senses at points where its meaning was decisive in his argument. The property for the protection of which men oblige themselves to civil society is sometimes (e.g., §§ 123, 131, 137) stated to be "life, liberty and estate," but sometimes (e.g., §§ 138–140) it is clearly only goods or land.[12] Consequently, men without estate or goods, that is, without property in the ordinary sense, are rightfully both in civil society and not in civil society.

When the property for the protection of which men enter civil society is taken to be life, liberty and estate, all men (except slaves) are eligible for membership; when it is taken to be goods or estate alone, then only men who possess them are eligible. Locke interprets it both ways, without any consciousness of inconsistency. What has happened is understandable in the light of our analysis. Locke's recognition of differential class rights in his own society, having been carried into his postulates as an implicit assumption of differential natural rights and rationality, without displacing the formal assumption of general rationality and equal rights, has emerged at the level of the social contract in a crucial ambiguity about who are parties to the contract.

The question as to whom Locke considered to be members of civil society seems to admit only one answer. Everyone, whether or not he has property in the ordinary sense, is included, as having an interest in preserving his life and liberty. At the same time only those with "estate" can be full members, for two reasons: only they have a full interest in the preservation of property, and only they are fully capable of that rational life—that voluntary obligation to the law of reason—which is the necessary basis for full participation in civil society. The laboring class, being without estate, are subject to, but not full members of, civil society. If it be objected that this is not one answer but two inconsistent answers, the reply must be that both answers follow from Locke's assumptions, and that neither one alone, but only the two together, accurately represent his thinking.

This ambiguity about membership in civil society by virtue of the supposed original contract allows Locke to consider all men as mem-

[12] A striking instance of the latter use is in § 138, where, after arguing that men in society must have property (since the purpose of their entering society was to preserve property), he concludes that "they have such a right to the goods which by the law of the community are theirs, that nobody hath a right to take their substance or any part of it from them without their own consent; without this they have no property at all."

bers for purposes of being ruled and only the men of estate as members for purposes of ruling. The right to rule (more accurately, the right to control any government) is given only to the men of estate; it is they who are given the decisive voice about taxation, without which no government can subsist (§ 140). On the other hand, the obligation to be bound by law and subject to the lawful government is fixed on all men whether or not they have property in the sense of estate, indeed, whether or not they have made an express compact. When Locke broadens his doctrine of express consent into a doctrine of tacit consent, he leaves no doubt about who are obligated. Tacit consent is assumed to have been given by "every man, that hath any possessions, or enjoyment, of any part of the dominions of any government . . . whether this his possession be of land, to him and his heirs forever, or a lodging only for a week; or whether it be barely travelling freely on the highway; and in effect, it reaches as far as the very being of any one within the territories of that government" (§ 119). Locke is careful to say (§ 122) that this does not make a man a full member of civil society, but only subjects him rightfully to its government: the men of no estate are not admitted to full membership by the back door of tacit consent. Of course, Locke had to retreat to tacit consent because it was impossible to show express consent in the case of present citizens of an established state. However, his doctrine of tacit consent has the added convenience that it clearly imposes obligation, reaching to their "very being," on those with no estate whatever.

It appears from the foregoing analysis that the result of Locke's work was to provide a moral basis for a class state from postulates of equal individual natural rights. Given the seventeenth-century individualist natural-rights assumptions, a class state could only be legitimized by a doctrine of consent which would bring one class within, but not make it fully a part of, the state. Locke's theory achieved this end. Its accomplishment required the implicit assumptions which he held. These assumptions involved him in the ambiguities and contradictions that pervade his argument. It is difficult to see how he could have persisted in such contradictions had he not been taking the class state as one desideratum and equal natural rights as another.

Locke did not twist deliberately a theory of equal natural rights into a justification for a class state. On the contrary, his honestly held natural-rights assumptions made it possible, indeed almost guaranteed, that his theory would justify a class state without any sleight of hand.

The decisive factor was that the equal natural rights Locke envisaged, including as they did the right to unlimited accumulation of property, led logically to differential class rights and so to justification of a class state. Locke's confusions are the result of honest deduction from a postulate of equal natural rights which contained its own contradiction. The evidence suggests that he did not realize the contradiction in the postulate of equal natural right to unlimited property, but that he simply read into the realm of right (or the state of nature) a social relation which he accepted as normal in civilized society. The source of the contradictions in his theory is his attempt to state in universal (nonclass) terms, rights and obligations which necessarily had a class content.

THE ENLIGHTENMENT: A BOURGEOIS IDEOLOGY *

Harold J. Laski

Harold J. Laski (1893–1950) was for many years professor of political science at the London School of Economics. His numerous writings cover almost all areas of political theory and government, A Grammar of Politics *(London: George Allen and Unwin, 1925), being the most comprehensive. He was a member of the Executive Committee of the Labour Party from 1936 to 1949 and its Chairman from 1945 to 1946.*

. . . Eighteenth century France is a society in ferment, and the pressure of new ideas is inexhaustible. The *ancien régime* was challenged in the name of new ideas. All the genius of the period was on the side of the novelties; its outlook permeated even those who had most to lose by its victory. The system could not meet the challenge. To the new ideas it opposed an outworn discipline the sanctions of which were

* Reprinted by permission of the publisher from Harold J. Laski, *The Rise of European Liberalism*, London: George Allen & Unwin Ltd., 1936, pp. 162–163, 211–224.

destroyed by its association with bankruptcy at home and defeat abroad. The monarchy was, at long last, compelled to take counsel with the middle class; and when it refused to accept the terms which the latter proffered, the result was its overthrow. As in the England of the Puritan rebellion, it was discovered that traditional institutions cannot be uprooted without a conflagration. Just as Hampden and Pym begat Lilburne and Winstanley, so Mirabeau and Mounier, in their turn, begat Babeuf and the *Enragés*. As Cromwell made possible the new equilibrium of the Restoration, so Napoleon made effective the compromise of the Charter. As 1688 made an England in which the middle class established their title to a predominant share in statehood, so, after a generation of passionate conflict, 1815 gave the French bourgeoisie their letters of credit. Meanwhile, in America, a middle-class state had, if in exceptional circumstances, been founded. The history of the nineteenth century is the record of the use made by that class of a power which it elevated to a universal plane. . . .

The outstanding feature of English political thought in the eighteenth century is the absence of any original note. Men were too satisfied with their achievements to go outside the well-worn lines of tradition; even the radicals go back directly to the mainstream of seventeenth century liberalism. In France, the reverse is the case. We have a political philosophy so luxuriant in its range of variation that no single generalization can do it adequate justice. There is a liberal conservatism, as with Montesquieu. There is a Utopian communism, built upon an ethical defence of equality, of which Mably and Morellet are the best-known, but by no means the only, representatives. Meslier stands alone as a convinced and relentless revolutionist; but there is a curious link between the foundations of his ideas and that economic determinism the pessimist character of which made Linguet a reactionary because he did not dare to hope. Rousseau stands apart from them all. Radical in theory, with even a proletarian nuance to his thinking, in positive recommendations he added little to his time. It was his special genius less to determine what men thought in matters of social constitution than to disturb their minds so profoundly as to provide new foundations for their thinking. He incarnated in himself all the dissatisfaction and discontent of his time. He taught men to see their wrongs with new intensity. But it is not easy to say whether his influence, as a whole, was radical or conservative. If Marat and Robespierre were his pupils in one generation, Hegel and Savigny were among the greatest of his disciples in the next, and the link between him and the romantic reaction is, of course, direct and profound. Here, as invariably in history, the search for any simple formula is bound to do violence to the facts.

Yet the most characteristic representative of French political thought in the age is Voltaire. Here, as so often, he invented nothing; but here, as so often also, he typified the mind of his time with remarkable accuracy. He was typical of its temper in his sense that great events were impending. He was typical, also, in his passion less for the foundations for politics than for the concrete remedy of concrete wrong. Voltaire is the social reformer *par excellence,* careless about consistency and system-making, eager to achieve immediate practical results. He is the broker of ideas, and not the architect of a system. Aware though he is of the importance of general ideas, he shrank from the price of their applications. Tolerant, invincibly liberal, eclectic, there was something in him which warned him always that politics is a philosophy of the second best. At the back of his mind was always the sense that too high a price might be paid for the logic of justice. He was a man of property, to whom the preservation of order was nature's first law. He was anxious for those improvements which might take place without risk to the foundations of the state. He recognized, with that sensitivity to the atmosphere which is not the least of his great qualities, that the foundations about him were undermined. That is why he was unready for any social philosophy which might add to the dangers he perceived.

It is, of course, true that, in an essential sense, politics proper was a secondary matter to Voltaire. The changes he recommended were always urged in the background of his own insistence that "je n'entre point dans la politique . . . la politique n'est pas mon affaire, je me suis toujours borné a faire mes petits efforts pour rendre les hommes moins sots et plus honnêtes".* That is of the inner reality of Voltaire. He is concerned not with the making of an ideology but the achievement of possible improvements. He had almost Burke's contempt for men who make political systems from the armchair of their study. To attack fanaticism and superstition, to fight for reforms which stand some chance of realization, this is how he conceived his task. If he did not refrain, on occasion, from theorizing, that was never the side of his work in which he took the greatest interest; it is even plain that it is in

* "I do enter into politics . . . politics are not my business. I have always limited my small efforts to making men less stupid and more decent."

their preoccupation with general ideas that he found the main weakness of Montesquieu and Rousseau. Voltaire represents, at its best, the normal outlook of the good and humane bourgeois of his generation who recognizes the existence of profound wrong and is eager for improvement consistently with safety to his own well-being. But at the back of his mind there is always a fear of going too far in the direction of change, a dread that, once the floodgates are opened, nothing may be left standing as the tide sweeps through. He seeks accordingly, for terms of accommodation that will fit the immediate necessities. He shuts his mind to profounder issues he is too fearful to face.

He sees no case against republicanism or democracy, though he thinks men rarely worthy to govern themselves. He knows that the French system degrades the stature of man; "a citizen of Amsterdam", he wrote, "is a man; a citizen a few miles distant therefrom is no more than a beast of burden". But he is profoundly monarchist so far as France is concerned, and he feared the tyranny of the lawyer more than he feared the tyranny of the King. "I would rather", he told St. Lambert, "obey a fine lion which is born far stronger than I than two hundred rats of my own species." He wants, of course, civil liberty on the English model; he never confounds monarchy with despotism. A constitutional system like that of England, "royalist republican" as he termed it, would have satisfied his main political aspirations.

But if Voltaire cares passionately for civil liberty under a constitutional system, he is also the great proprietor with a scrupulous regard to his rights as such. He hates religious fanaticism; but he is certain that religion is necessary for the people if the rich are not to be murdered in their beds. We need the conception of a God who rewards the good and punishes the evil for social purposes. "Je veux," he wrote in the *A.B.C.*, "que mon procureur, mon tailleur, ma femme même croient en Dieu, et je m'imagine que j'en serai mons volé et moins cocu." * The god of Voltaire is a social necessity for the maintenance of order; without him there would be no restraint upon the behaviour of men. "Quel autre frein", he wrote, "pouvait-on mettre à la cupidité, aux transgressions secrètes et impunies, que l'idée d'un maître éternel qui nous voit et qui jugera jusqu'a nos plus secrèts pensées." † It was for the same

* "I want my lawyer, my tailor, and even my wife to believe in God; for I imagine that I shall then not be robbed or cuckholded so much."

† "What other bridle could one put on cupidity, on secret transgressors and impunities, than the idea of an eternal master who sees, and who will judge, even our most secret thoughts."

reason that he preached both freedom of the will and the immortality of the soul. As metaphysical principles he accepted neither; but, as he told Helvetius, social considerations made it urgent that both should be defended as though they were in fact true.

In any essential sense, Voltaire has no use for equality. Equal property is a mere chimaera; it could only be attained by unjust spoliation. "It is impossible", he wrote, "in our unhappy world for men living in society not to be divided into the two classes of rich and poor." Without the poor, indeed, there could be no civilization; it is because men have to work that society can survive. We are not equally talented, and property, in general, is a return to talent. To pretend that men are equally members of society, that, as Jean Jacques said, a sovereign should be willing to marry his son to the executioner's daughter is simply the charlatanry of a savage. Subordination is a social necessity; and the rich repay society by the opportunities they open to the poor. In any case, the relation of riches to happiness is greatly exaggerated, for a shepherd is often happier than a king. We ought to give the poor the chance of growing rich; but more than this is unnecessary.

For the common people, indeed, he has profound contempt; they are the source of all fanaticism and superstition. If sometimes he writes with enthusiasm about the possibilities of national education, for the most part he does not think it worth while. The "canaille"—the "swinish multitude" of Burke—is not "worthy" of enlightenment. He congratulated La Chalotais in prohibiting educational studies to the working man. "On my land", he wrote, "I want labourers and not tonsured clerics." He told Damilaville that the perpetuation of the uninstructed masses was essential and that anyone who owned property and needed servants would think the same; and he wrote to d'Alembert that any effort spent on instructing the servant and the shoemaker was simply a waste of time. So long as men like the philosophers were free to speculate, it did not matter if the tailor and the grocer remained under the domination of the church. He was, indeed, afraid of the social consequences of popular enlightenment; "when the people meddles with argument", he wrote, "everything is lost". It is true that he wants, little by little, the power of reason to extend from important citizens to the poorer classes, and that, in a letter to Linguet, he seems to believe that the skilled artisan is capable of instruction. But the essence of Voltaire is a profound respect for the established order whose principles he is not willing to jeopardize by too drastic or too wide a scrutiny.

And this is the more apparent the more closely his programme of reform is examined. The changes he demanded were broadly those of the prosperous bourgeoisie. He wanted liberty; but he wanted, also, a liberty compatible with the fullest opportunities for men of property. Under the influence of Mandeville, he wrote an ardent defence of luxury. He saw in the growth of commerce a social benefit indifferently to the distribution of its results. He objected to sumptuary legislation as a violation of the rights of property. His case against the church is largely founded on the incompatibility between its discipline and national prosperity. His interest in the poor does not extend far beyond a compassionate desire for the more obvious ameliorations of their lot. There is nothing in him of that passionate indignation against an unjust social order which is the clue to all Rousseau's thinking; he never, even, had those moments Diderot knew in which he was prepared to doubt whether a man of feeling could ever approve the irrationalism of social life. The world he wanted to build was, of course, an infinitely better world than the one he inherited. But the improvements would have been limited in their benefit very much to the propertied class. His liberalism, as an active and consistent principle, did not penetrate beyond their needs.

And this is true of the main body of thinkers associated with the movement he led. There is, no doubt, a profound radical in Diderot; but this is, with him, an inconstant and emotional outbreak rather than a considered intellectual principle. He attacked Helvetius' proposals for the diminution of inequality; they would, he said, injure property and destroy all industry. He had contempt for the common man. "L'homme peuple", he wrote, "est le plus sot et le plus méchant de tous les hommes; se dépopulariser ou se rendre meilleur, c'est la même chose." * He makes the rights of property almost as absolute as may well be imagined. "Men in society who have property", he wrote, "have a portion of the general wealth of which he is absolute master, over which he has the powers of a king to use or abuse at his discretion. A private citizen may cultivate his land or not as he pleases without the government having any right to interfere in the matter. For if the government deals with abuses of property, it will not be slow to deal with its uses as well. When that happens, there is an end to any true notion of property or liberty." His enthusiasm for Mercier de la Rivière

* "The man of the people is the most stupid and most wicked of men; to cease being one and to improve oneself are one and the same thing."

is well known; and his general respect for the Physiocrats was undeviating. He differs, indeed, from Voltaire in his dislike of luxury and his refusal to believe that poverty and happiness were easily compatible. There are even bitter attacks on the injustice of the contemporary social order which almost reflect the spirit of Rousseau. But, in general, the economic outlook of Diderot was very much that of the Physiocrats. He felt sentimentally for the poor; but he had no criticism to make of the general contours of liberal economic doctrine.

This conclusion must, I think, remain unaffected by the import of such essays as the *Entretien de l'aumonier et d'Orou* or the more famous *Supplément au voyage de Bougainville* in which Diderot seems to outdistance Rousseau in his attack upon the foundations of civilized society. For even when they are read in conjunction with some of his more radical articles in the *Encyclopedia* they amount to little more than a pious hope that things will be better. Progressive taxation, a more equitable distribution of wealth, less luxury, a greater tenderness for the poor, a wider attention to education, it is difficult to see in Diderot's programme very much more than this. The sage in the Supplément does not ask for any fundamental change. "We shall attack bad laws", says Diderot, "until they are reformed; meanwhile let us obey them. He who of his own private authority infringes a bad law authorizes everyone to infringe the good. There is less inconvenience in being mad with madmen than being alone in one's wisdom."

What, indeed, has been called the socialism of Diderot is, at bottom, nothing more than the feeling of doubt every sensitive and generous mind must have at the grim contrasts with which society presents us. It leads Diderot to make a gesture of moral protest against their result; it does not lead him to more. Much of the same may fairly be said of Helvetius. Though his remark that work in moderation is no more difficult for the poor to support than is ennui for the rich suggests that the social problem was, for Helvetius, an intellectual problem felt in a superficial way—the kindly compassion of a *grand seigneur* —he is uneasy about the conditions he confronts. He dislikes luxury and a too great inequality of economic condition; he argues that they lead to the ruin of states. But he has no remedy to suggest save an extension of proprietorship, and he has no method whereby to achieve this end save by hoping that wise legislation will secure it. He thinks it would be just to redistribute the ownership of the land; but such a scheme "is inconvenient because it violates the right to property which is the most sacred of all laws". Property, he writes, is "the moral god of empires". It makes possible the unity of a state. It is one of those laws without which society cannot be preserved. What, therefore, we should aim at is equality of happiness, and in a well-governed country this is fortunately attainable without any basic change in the nature of economic arrangements.

Helvetius is a liberal unprepared to confront the price of change; the Baron d'Holbach is, in essential political principle, conservative in outlook. He may admit, like so many of his generation, that the system of government is wholly evil, so evil that it makes men criminals despite themselves. He agrees that luxury should be restrained. True wealth in a state, he says, consists in the comfort of the many, not the opulence of the few. It is more important that the people should have bread than that a monarch should have his gorgeously furnished palaces. There is always a tendency in every society for the rich to grasp at all they can. He wants more charity, and workshops in which the laborious poor may find the means to live. But he favours inequality. He thinks that division between rich and poor is inevitable. He is afraid of any measures that may attack or endanger the sacred principle of private property. At bottom, it is not unfair to say that while the spectacle of social misery causes him discomfort, he has no more than a moral gesture to make about its consequences. Like most thinkers of his time, he has been profoundly affected by Rousseau's assault upon the adequacy of social foundations. But his response to Rousseau's challenge occupies a very limited place in his work, and it is enough for him to signalize the existence of the evil without attempting any profound or systematic search for the remedies.

And this attitude, it may be said, is broadly characteristic of the time. It is no doubt true that there is immense preoccupation with social problems; on the problem of the poor alone there exists a vast literature full of deep feeling and no little inventive ingenuity. But any analysis of this literature reveals no desire to grapple with the central issue of private property. There are eulogies and to spare of the spirit of equality and of the duty of the rich to be generous to the poor; it is notable, for instance, that the Archbishop of Paris had to rebuke some of his clergy for excessive radicalism in this regard. There is even a number of plans, some worked out in great detail, for the construction of national workshops in which the unemployed poor could find a living; but these are always, even with the most radical, built upon the principle that the wages paid in them must never be at such a level as to interfere with the demands of private enterprise. The poor, in a word, are to pay the price of their poverty. The liberal thinkers of the time are anxious to mitigate their poverty; but that is the limit of their effort. Even where, as with Mably, they defend a communist framework of social organization, this is always in the background of a virtual admission that they are outlining an impossible dream. Even, again, when Linguet depicts with relentless clarity the roots of the *malaise* from which civilization is suffering and predicts that, from the misery of the poor, a new Spartacus will arise, he has no remedies to suggest. He praises the despotism of the Orient because, securing as it does a blind obedience from the people, it preserves the safety of the state. He told Voltaire that in his view a knowledge of arts and letters is dangerous for the working class. "The condition of society", he wrote to the latter, "condemns him to the use of his physical strength alone. Everything would be lost once he knew that he had a mind." Linguet, in a word, foresaw that social injustice implied inevitable catastrophe; but he did not know how to prevent it, and he was convinced that no good could come of the destruction of the old order. He tears aside the veil which conceals its monstrosities more vigorously and more relentlessly than any Frenchman save Meslier before the Revolution. But when his analysis is done, he can do no more than throw up his hands.

The French critics of the *ancien régime,* in short, sought to accomplish two things. France needed a constitution which would redress the balance between an outworn political system, and a new distribution of economic power; they sought, with unsurpassed energy, to trace the outlines of what that system should be. They sought, also, in building the new system to release its cultural foundations from the prison in which organized religion still sought to confine them. They were hostile to the church and the aristocracy; they were critical of those who lived on society without labouring on its behalf; they were sympathetic, often generous, to the sufferings of the poor. But they were not seriously prepared to confront the problem of the poor except in terms of charity. They were unable to discern behind the Third Estate a Fourth with claims as wide as, and interests different from, those of the bourgeoisie. They assumed that their own emancipation implied also advantages to the workers, and they were content with that. They saw no way in which the problem of poverty could be solved and, charity apart, they averted their eyes from it. Voltaire summarized their effective attitude with his usual precision. "It is inevitable", he wrote in the *Philosophic Dictionary,* "that mankind should be divided into two classes with many sub-divisions—the oppressors and the oppressed. Fortunately, use and wont and the lack of leisure prevent most of the oppressed from realizing their condition. When they do feel it, civil war follows which can end only in the enslavement of the people, since the sovereign power in the state is money." Another passage in the *Siècle de Louis XIV* emphasizes the same attitude. "The labourer and the artisan", Voltaire wrote, "must be cut down to necessaries, if they are to work: this is human nature. It is inevitable that the majority should be poor; it is only not necessary that it should be wretched."

An eminent critic has remarked that no one can read Voltaire's discussion of the economic problem without the sense that he is uncomfortable at his own conclusions. That explains both his evasions and his cynicism, the absence from his analysis of that noble indignation he displays whenever it is intolerance he has to attack. The remark is a just one; though it should be added that its application is not limited to Voltaire. All French liberalism of the eighteenth century is permeated by a similar temper. Its exponents were demanding in effect the emancipation of the whole nation; but when they applied themselves to the details of their programme their imagination limited its range to the freedoms sought by men of property. Farther than this they were not prepared to go. Their justification is a complicated one. In part, as they would have explained, if they avoided the issue of justice, they confronted the obligation to be generous; provision for the poor by the state plays a large part in all their discussions. In part, again, they were overwhelmingly individualist in temper. The state they knew was arbitrary, corrupt, incompetent. They sought to free themselves from its control, to trace out limits to its activities, not to fall again under its domination in a new form. In part, also, they feared and distrusted the working class. They feared its ignorance and its savagery; they distrusted its ability to make a contribution of value to the state. They themselves, from nothing, had become everything; it seemed to them that their obligation to society was above all the translation of their moral claims into legal rights. They set out their case in universal terms, because they needed, like the English reformers of 1832, the support of the working class if they were to triumph. But they no more conceived that their victory could mean the emancipation of that class than did the English reformers half a century later. Their view was intelligible enough when we bear in mind that not until the middle of the nineteenth century were the workers organically conscious of their claims. A class enters into history only when it is a plaintiff in its court. In the eighteenth century, the bourgeoisie alone was in this position; and the thinkers were rare who could see that the conquest of its revolutionary demands would be a stage only, and not the term, of human development. French liberalism, with great power and insight, formulated the demands of the new claimant to human rights without seeing that when they had been satisfied, they would merely set the conditions of a new conflict. But it is the way of history to blind men's visions to the destiny of man's effort. Perhaps he travels a longer distance because he has no foreknowledge of the end of his journey.

THE MENTALITY OF A VICTORIOUS MIDDLE CLASS *

Louis Hartz

Louis Hartz is professor of government at Harvard where he teaches modern American and European political theory. His most recent work, on comparative culture, is The Founding of New Societies *(New York: Harcourt, Brace & World, 1965).*

When the Americans celebrated the uniqueness of their own society, they were on the track of a personal insight of the profoundest importance. For the nonfeudal world in which they lived shaped every aspect of their social thought: it gave them a frame of mind that cannot be found anywhere else in the eighteenth century, or in the wider history of modern revolutions.

One of the first things it did was to breed a set of revolutionary

* Extracts from *The Liberal Tradition in America,* (pp. 39–41, 43–51, 53–55), copyright, 1955, by Louis Hartz. Reprinted by permission of Harcourt, Brace & World, Inc.

thinkers in America who were human beings like Otis and Adams rather than secular prophets like Robespierre and Lenin. Despite the European flavor of a Jefferson or a Franklin, the Americans refused to join in the great Enlightenment enterprise of shattering the Christian concept of sin, replacing it with an unlimited humanism, and then emerging with an earthly paradise as glittering as the heavenly one that had been destroyed. The fact that the Americans did not share the crusading spirit of the French and the Russians, as we have seen, is already some sort of confirmation of this, for that spirit was directly related to the "civil religion" of Europe and is quite unthinkable without it. Nor is it hard to see why the liberal good fortune of the Americans should have been at work in the position they held. Europe's brilliant dream of an impending millennium, like the mirage of a thirstridden man, was inspired in large part by the agonies it experienced. When men have already inherited the freest society in the world, and are grateful for it, their thinking is bound to be a solider type. America has been a sober nation, but it has also been a comfortable one, and the two points are by no means unrelated.

Sam Adams, for example, rejects the hope of changing human nature: in a mood of Calvinist gloom, he traces the tyranny of England back to "passions of Men" that are fixed and timeless. But surely it would be unreasonable to congratulate him for this approach without observing that he implicitly confines those passions to the political sphere—the sphere of parliaments, ministers, and stampmasters—and thus leaves a social side to man which can be invoked to hold him in check. The problem was a different one for Rousseau and Marx, who started from the view that the corruption of man was complete, as wide as the culture in which he lived, with the result that revolutions became meaningless unless they were based on the hope of changing him. Here, obviously, is a place where the conclusions of political thought breathe a different spirit from the assumptions on which they rest. Behind the shining optimism of Europe, there are a set of anguished grievances; behind the sad resignation of America, a set of implicit satisfactions.

One of these satisfactions, moreover, was crucially important in developing the sober temper of the American revolutionary outlook. It was the high degree of religious diversity that prevailed in colonial life. This meant that the revolution would be led in part by fierce Dissenting ministers, and their leadership destroyed the chance for a conflict to arise between the worldly pessimism of Christianity and the worldly ambitions of revolutionary thought. In Europe, especially on the continent, where reactionary church establishments had made the Christian concept of sin and salvation into an explicit pillar of the status quo, liberals were forced to develop a political religion—as Rousseau saw—if only in answer to it. The Americans not only avoided this compulsion; they came close, indeed, to reversing it. Here, above all in New England, the clergy was so militant that it was Tories like Daniel Leonard who were reduced to blasting it as a dangerous "political engine," a situation whose irony John Adams caught when he reminded Leonard that "in all ages and countries" the church is "disposed enough" to be on the side of conservatism. Thus the American liberals, instead of being forced to pull the Christian heaven down to earth, were glad to let it remain where it was. They did not need to make a religion out of the revolution because religion was already revolutionary. . . . Sir William Ashley, discussing the origins of the "American spirit," once remarked that "as feudalism was not transplanted to the New World, there was no need for the strong arm of a central power to destroy it." This is a simple statement but, like many of Ashley's simple statements, it contains a neglected truth. For Americans usually assume that their attack on political power in 1776 was determined entirely by the issues of the revolution, when as a matter of fact it was precisely because of the things they were not revolting against that they were able to carry it through. The action of England inspired the American colonists with a hatred of centralized authority; but had that action been a transplanted American feudalism, rich in the chaos of ages, then they would surely have had to dream of centralizing authority themselves.

They would, in other words, have shared the familiar agony of European liberalism—hating power and loving it too. The liberals of Europe in the eighteenth century wanted, of course, to limit power; but confronted with the heritage of an ancient corporate society, they were forever devising sharp and sovereign instruments that might be used to put it down. Thus while the Americans were attacking Dr. Johnson's theory of sovereignty, one of the most popular liberal doctrines in Europe, cherished alike by Bentham and Voltaire, was the doctrine of the enlightened despot, a kind of political deism in which a single force would rationalize the social world. While the Americans were praising the "illustrious Montesquieu" for his idea of checks and balances, that worthy was under heavy attack in France itself because he compromised the unity of power on which so many liberals relied. Even the English Whigs, men who were by no means believers in monarchical absolutism, found it impossible to go along with their eager young friends across the Atlantic. When the Americans, closing their eyes to 1688, began to lay the ax to the concept of parliamentary sovereignty, most of the Whigs fled their company at once.

A philosopher, it is true, might look askance at the theory of power the Americans developed. It was not a model of lucid exposition. The trouble lay with their treatment of sovereignty. Instead of boldly rejecting the concept, as Franklin was once on the verge of doing when he said that it made him "quite sick," they accepted the concept and tried to qualify it out of existence. The result was a chaotic series of forays and retreats in which a sovereign Parliament was limited, first by the distinction between external and internal taxation, then by the distinction between revenue and regulation, and finally by the remarkable contention that colonial legislatures were as sovereign as Parliament was. But there is a limit to how much we can criticize the Americans for shifting their ground. They were obviously feeling their way; and they could hardly be expected to know at the time of the Stamp Act what their position would be at the time of the First Continental Congress. Moreover, if they clung to the concept of sovereignty, they battered it beyond belief, and no one would confuse their version of it with the one advanced by Turgot or even by Blackstone in Europe. The meekness of the American sovereign testifies to the beating he had received. Instead of putting up a fierce and embarrassing battle against the limits of natural law and the separation of powers, as he usually did in the theories of Europe, he accepted those limits with a vast docility.

If we look at what happened to America's famous idea of judicial control when the physiocrats advanced it in France, we will get an insight into this whole matter. Who studies now the theory of legal guardianship with which La Rivière tried to bind down his rational and absolute sovereign? Who indeed remembers it? American students of the judicial power rarely go to Cartesian France to discover a brother of James Otis—and the reason is evident enough. When the physiocrats appealed to the courts, they were caught at once in a vise of criticism: either they were attacked for reviving the feudal idea of the *parlements* or they were blasted as insincere because they had originally advanced a despot to deal with the feudal problem. They had to give the idea up.

But in America, where the social questions of France did not exist and the absolutism they engendered was quite unthinkable, the claim of Otis in the Writs of Assistance Case, that laws against reason and the Constitution were "void" and that the "Courts must pass them into disuse," met an entirely different fate. It took root, was carried forward by a series of thinkers, and blossomed ultimately into one of the most remarkable institutions in modern politics.

The question, again, was largely a question of the free society in which the Americans lived. Nor ought we to assume that its impact on their view of political power disappeared when war and domestic upheaval finally came. Of course, there was scattered talk of the need for a "dictator," as Jefferson angrily reported in 1782; and until new assemblies appeared in most places, committees of public safety had authoritarian power. But none of this went deep enough to shape the philosophic mood of the nation. A hero is missing from the revolutionary literature of America. He is the legislator, the classical giant who almost invariably turns up at revolutionary moments to be given authority to lay the foundations of the free society. He is not missing because the Americans were unfamiliar with images of ancient history, or because they had not read the Harringtons or the Machiavellis and Rousseaus of the modern period. Harrington, as a matter of fact, was one of their favorite writers. The legislator is missing because, in truth, the Americans had no need for his services. Much as they liked Harrington's republicanism, they did not require a Cromwell, as Harrington thought he did, to erect the foundations for it. Those foundations had already been laid by history.

The issue of history itself is deeply involved here. On this score, inevitably, the fact that the revolutionaries of 1776 had inherited the freest society in the world shaped their thinking in an intricate way. It gave them, in the first place, an appearance of outright conservatism. We know, of course, that most liberals of the eighteenth century, from Bentham to Quesnay, were bitter opponents of history, posing a sharp antithesis between nature and tradition. And it is an equally familiar fact that their adversaries, including Burke and Blackstone, sought to break down this antithesis by identifying natural law with the slow evolution of the past. The militant Americans, confronted with these two positions, actually took the second. Until Jefferson raised the banner of independence, and even in many cases after that time, they based their claims on a philosophic synthesis of Anglo-American legal history and the reason of natural law. Blackstone, the very Blackstone whom Bentham so bitterly attacked in the very year 1776, was a rock on which they relied.

The explanation is not hard to find. The past had been good to the Americans, and they knew it. Instead of inspiring them to the fury of Bentham and Voltaire, it often produced a mystical sense of Providential guidance akin to that of Maistre—as when Rev. Samuel West, surveying the growth of America's population, anticipated victory in the revolution because "we have been prospered in a most wonderful manner." The troubles they had with England did not alter this outlook. Even these, as they pointed out again and again, were of recent origin, coming after more than a century of that "salutary neglect" which Burke defended so vigorously. And in a specific sense, of course, the record of English history in the seventeenth century and the record of colonial charters from the time of the Virginia settlement provided excellent ammunition for the battle they were waging in defense of colonial rights. A series of circumstances had conspired to saturate even the revolutionary position of the Americans with the quality of traditionalism—to give them, indeed, the appearance of outraged reactionaries. "This I call an innovation," thundered John Dickinson, in his attack on the Stamp Act, "a most dangerous innovation."

Now here was a frame of mind that would surely have troubled many of the illuminated liberals in Europe, were it not for an ironic fact. America piled on top of this paradox another one of an opposite kind and thus, by misleading them twice as it were, gave them a deceptive sense of understanding.

Actually, the form of America's traditionalism was one thing, its content quite another. Colonial history had not been the slow and glacial record of development that Bonald and Maistre loved to talk about. On the contrary, since the first sailing of the *Mayflower*, it had been a story of new beginnings, daring enterprises, and explicitly stated principles—it breathed, in other words, the spirit of Bentham himself. The result was that the traditionalism of the Americans, like a pure freak of logic, often bore amazing marks of antihistorical rationalism. The clearest case of this undoubtedly is to be found in the revolutionary constitutions of 1776, which evoked, as Franklin reported, the "rapture" of European liberals everywhere. In America, of course, the concept of a written constitution, including many of the mechanical devices it embodied, was the end-product of a chain of historical experience that went back to the Mayflower Compact and the Plantation Covenants of the New England towns: it was the essence of political traditionalism. But in Europe just the reverse was true. The concept was the darling of the rationalists—a symbol of the emancipated mind at work. . . .

But how then are we to describe these baffling Americans? Were they rationalists or were they traditionalists? The truth is, they were neither, which is perhaps another way of saying that they were both. For the war between Burke and Bentham on the score of tradition, which made a great deal of sense in a society where men had lived in the shadow of feudal institutions, made comparatively little sense in a society where for years they had been creating new states, planning new settlements, and, as Jefferson said, literally building new lives. In such a society a strange dialectic was fated to appear, which would somehow unite the antagonistic components of the European mind; the past became a continuous future, and the God of the traditionalists sanctioned the very arrogance of the men who defied Him.

This shattering of the time categories of Europe, this Hegelian-like revolution in historic perspective, goes far to explain one of the enduring secrets of the American character: a capacity to combine rock-ribbed traditionalism with high inventiveness, ancestor worship with ardent optimism. Most critics have seized upon one or the other of these aspects of the American mind, finding it impossible to conceive how both can go together. That is why the insight of Gunnar Myrdal is a very distinguished one when he writes: "America is . . . conservative. . . . But the principles conserved are liberal and some, indeed, are radical." Radicalism and conservatism have been twisted entirely out of shape by the liberal flow of American history.

What I have been doing here is fairly evident: I have been interpreting the social thought of the American revolution in terms of the social goals *it did not need to achieve*. Given the usual approach, this may seem like a perverse inversion of the reasonable course of things; but in a world where the "canon and feudal law" are missing, how else are we to understand the philosophy of a liberal revolution? The remarkable thing about the "spirit of 1776," as we have seen, is not that it sought emancipation but that it sought it in a sober temper; not that it opposed power but that it opposed it ruthlessly and continuously; not that it looked forward to the future but that it worshiped the past as well. Even these perspectives, however, are only part of the story, misleading in themselves. The "free air" of American life, as John Jay once happily put it, penetrated to deeper levels of the American mind, twisting it in strange ways, producing a set of results fundamental to everything else in American thought. The clue to these results lies in the following fact: the Americans, though models to all the world of the middle class way of life, lacked the passionate middle class consciousness which saturated the liberal thought of Europe. . . .

. . . Fundamental aspects of Europe's bourgeois code of political thought met an ironic fate in the most bourgeois country in the world. They were not so much rejected as they were ignored, treated indifferently, because the need for their passionate affirmation did not exist. Physiocratic economics is an important case in point. Where economic parasites are few, why should men embark on a passionate search for the productive laborer? Where guild restrictions are comparatively slight and continental tariffs unknown, why should they embrace the ruthless atomism of Turgot? America's attack on the English Acts of Trade was couched in terms of Locke, not in terms of Quesnay; and though Franklin and Jefferson were much taken by the "modern economics," they did not, here as in certain other places, voice the dominant preoccupation of American thought. It had often been said, of course, that the Americans were passionately laissez faire in their thinking, but this is to confuse either bourgeois ease with bourgeois frustration or a hatred of absolute power with the very economic atomism which, in physiocratic terms, was allied to it. Turgot himself saw that the Americans did not long to smash a feudal world into economic atoms any more than they longed for a unified sovereign to accomplish this feat. A lover of the Americans who, like European liberals, could not quite imagine life outside the *ancien régime,* he complained bitterly on both counts. His complaint on the count of sovereignty is legendary, but his complaint on the count of laissez faire has, alas, been entirely forgotten. This is because John Adams replied to the one in his *Defence of the Constitutions* but did not mention the other. And yet it appears in the same place, in Turgot's famous letter to Richard Price: "*On suppose partout le droit de regler le commerce . . . tant on est loin d'avoir* *senti que la loi de la liberté de tout commerce est un corollaire du droit de propriété."* *

The lament of Turgot reveals that America's indifference to the bourgeois fixations of Europe had in itself a positive meaning: the failure to develop a physiocratic conscience led to a quiet and pragmatic outlook on the question of business controls. This is the outlook that characterizes a whole mass of early economic legislation that American historians are now beginning to unearth in what should have been, reputedly, the most "laissez faire" country in the world. But it is in connection with materialism and idealism, utilitarianism and natural law, that the inverted position of the Americans comes out most clearly. There was no Bentham, no Helvetius, among the superlatively middle-class American thinkers. On the contrary, they stuck with Puritan passion to the dogma of natural law, as if an outright hedonism were far too crass for consideration. In a purely political sense this may be interesting, because the Americans, at least during the Stamp Act phase of their struggle, were fighting that corrupt system of parliamentary representation which in England Benthamism later rose to assail. But it is in terms of the wider significance of utility as an attack on feudal norms, as an effort to make of "business a noble life," as Crane Brinton has put it, that America's indifference to it takes on its deepest meaning. Benjamin Franklins in fact, the Americans did not have to become Jeremy Benthams in theory. Unchallenged men of business, they did not have to equate morality with it. And this has been a lasting paradox in the history of American thought. The American tradition of natural law still flourishes after a century and a half of the most reckless material exploitation that the modern world has seen. A persistent idealism of mind, reflected in Emerson's remark that utilitarianism is a "stinking philosophy," has been one of the luxuries of a middle class that has never been forced to become class conscious.

* "Everywhere the right to regulate commerce is accepted . . . that is how far people are from recognizing that the law of free commerce is a corollary of the right to property."

THE CONSERVATIVE UTOPIA *

Karl Mannheim

Karl Mannheim (1893–1947) was professor at the University of Frankfurt a. M, until 1933 when Hitler forced him into exile. He then became a lecturer at the London School of Economics, and soon one of the most influential social theorists in the English-speaking world. Ideology and Utopia *is the most widely read of his many books.*

The mode of thought of bureaucratic conservatism will be considered first. The fundamental tendency of all bureaucratic thought is to turn all problems of politics into problems of administration. As a result, the majority of books on politics in the history of German political science are *de facto* treatises on administration. If we consider the role that bureaucracy has always played, especially in the Prussian state, and to what extent the intelligentsia was largely an intelligentsia drawn from the bureaucracy, this onesidedness of the history of political science in Germany becomes easily intelligible.

The attempt to hide all problems of politics under the cover of administration may be explained by the fact that the sphere of activity of the official exists only within the limits of laws already formulated. Hence the genesis or the development of law falls outside the scope of his activity. As a result of his socially limited horizon, the functionary fails to see that behind every law that has been made there lie the socially fashioned interests and the *Weltanschauungen* of a specific social group. He takes it for granted that the specific order prescribed by the concrete law is equivalent to order in general. He does not understand that every rationalized order is only one of many forms in which socially conflicting irrational forces are reconciled.

The administrative, legalistic mind has its own peculiar type of rationality. When faced with the play of hitherto unharnessed forces,

---

* Reprinted by permission of Routledge & Kegan Paul, Ltd., from Karl Mannheim, *Ideology and Utopia,* London: Kegan Paul, Trench, Trubner & Co., Ltd., 1936, pp. 105–108, 206–212.

as, for example, the eruption of collective energies in a revolution, it can conceive of them only as momentary disturbances. It is, therefore, no wonder that in every revolution the bureaucracy tries to find a remedy by means of arbitrary decrees rather than to meet the political situation on its own grounds. It regards revolution as an untoward event within an otherwise ordered system and not as the living expression of fundamental social forces on which the existence, the preservation, and the development of society depends. The juristic administrative mentality constructs only closed static systems of thought, and is always faced with the paradoxical task of having to incorporate into its system new laws, which arise out of the unsystematized interaction of living forces as if they were only a further elaboration of the original system. . . .

Every bureaucracy, therefore, in accord with the peculiar emphasis on its own position, tends to generalize its own experience and to overlook the fact that the realm of administration and of smoothly functioning order represents only a part of the total political reality. Bureaucratic thought does not deny the possibility of a science of politics, but regards it as identical with the science of administration. Thus irrational factors are overlooked, and when these nevertheless force themselves to the fore, they are treated as "routine matters of state." A classic expression of this standpoint is contained in a saying which originated in these circles: "A good administration is better than the best constitution."

In addition to bureaucratic conservatism, which ruled Germany and especially Prussia to a very great extent, there was a second type of conservatism which developed parallel to it and which may be called historical conservatism. It was peculiar to the social group of the nobility and the bourgeois strata among the intellectuals who were the intellectual and actual rulers of the country, but between whom and the bureaucratic conservatives there always existed a certain amount of tension. This mode of thought bore the stamp of the German universities, and especially of the dominant group of historians. Even to-day, this mentality still finds its support largely in these circles.

Historical conservatism is characterized by the fact that it is aware of that irrational realm in the life of the state which cannot be managed by administration. It recognizes that there is an unorganized and incalculable realm which is the proper sphere of politics. Indeed it focuses its attention almost exclusively on the impulsive, irrational factors which furnish the real basis for the further development of state and society. It regards these forces as entirely beyond comprehension and infers that, as such, human reason is impotent to understand or to control them. Here only a traditionally inherited instinct, "silently working" spiritual forces, the "folk spirit," *Volksgeist*, drawing their strength out of the depths of the unconscious, can be of aid in moulding the future.

This attitude was already stated at the end of the eighteenth century by Burke, who served as the model for most of the German conservatives, in the following impressive words: "The science of constructing a commonwealth or renovating it or reforming it, is like every other experimental science, not to be taught *a priori*. Nor is it a short experience that can instruct us in that practical science." The sociological roots of this thesis are immediately evident. It expressed the ideology of the dominant nobility in England and in Germany, and it served to legitimatize their claims to leadership in the state. The *je ne sais quoi* element in politics, which can be acquired only through long experience, and which reveals itself as a rule only to those who for many generations have shared in political leadership, is intended to justify government by an aristocratic class. This makes clear the manner in which the social interests of a given group make the members of that group sensitive to certain aspects of social life to which those in another position do not respond. Whereas the bureaucracy is blinded to the political aspect of a situation by reason of its administrative preconceptions, from the very beginning the nobility is perfectly at home in this sphere. Right from the start, the latter have their eyes on the arena where intra- and interstate spheres of power collide with one another. In this sphere, petty textbook wisdom deserts us and solutions to problems cannot be mechanically deduced from premises. Hence it is not individual intelligence which decides issues. Rather is every event the resultant of actual political forces.

The historical conservative theory, which is essentially the expression of a feudal tradition become self-conscious, is primarily concerned with problems which transcend the sphere of administration. The sphere is regarded as a completely irrational one which cannot be fabricated by mechanical methods but which grows of its own accord. This outlook relates everything to the decisive dichotomy between "construction according to calculated plan" and "allowing things to grow." For the political leader it is not sufficient to possess merely the correct knowledge and the mastery of certain laws and norms. In addition to these he must possess that inborn instinct, sharpened through long experience, which leads him to the right answer.

Two types of irrationalism have joined to produce this irrational way of thinking: on the one hand, precapitalistic, traditionalistic irrationalism (which regards legal thinking, for instance, as a way of sensing something and not as mechanical calculation), and, on the other hand, romantic irrationalism. A mode of thought is thus created which conceives of history as the reign of pre- and super-rational forces. Even Ranke, the most eminent representative of the historical school, spoke from this intellectual outlook when he defined the relations of theory and practice. Politics is not, according to him, an independent science that can be taught. The statesman may indeed study history profitably, but not in order to derive from it rules of conduct, but rather because it serves to sharpen his political instinct. This mode of thought may be designated as the ideology of political groups which have traditionally occupied a dominant position but which have rarely participated in the administrative bureaucracy. . . .

Conservative mentality as such has no predisposition towards theorizing. This is in accord with the fact that human beings do not theorize about the actual situations in which they live as long as they are well adjusted to them. They tend, under such conditions of existence, to regard the environment as part of a natural world-order which, consequently, presents no problems. Conservative mentality as such has no utopia. Ideally it is in its very structure completely in harmony with the reality which, for the time being, it has mastered. It lacks all those reflections and illuminations of the historical process which come from a progressive impulse. The conservative type of knowledge originally is the sort of knowledge giving practical control. It consists of habitual and often also of reflective orientations towards those factors which are immanent in the situation. There are ideal elements surviving in the present as hangovers from the tension of former periods in which the world was not yet stabilized and which operate now only ideologically as faiths, religions, and myths which have been banished to a realm beyond history. At this stage, thought, as we have indicated, inclines to accept the total environment in the accidental concreteness in which it occurs, as if it were the proper order of the world, to be taken for granted and presenting no problem. Only the counter-attack of opposing classes and their tendency to break through the limits of the existing order causes the conservative mentality to question the basis of its own dominance, and necessarily brings about among the conservatives historical-philosophical reflections concerning themselves. Thus, there arises a counter-utopia which serves as a means of self-orientation and defence.

If the socially ascendant classes had not in reality raised these problems and if they had not given them utterance in their respective counter-ideologies, the tendency of conservatism to become conscious of itself would have remained latent and the conservative outlook would have continued on a level of unconscious behaviour. But the ideological attack of a socially ascendant group representing a new epoch does, in fact, bring about an awareness of the attitudes and ideas which assert themselves only in life and in action. Goaded on by opposing theories, conservative mentality discovers its *idea* only *ex post facto*. It is no accident that whereas all progressive groups regard the idea as coming before the deed, for the conservative Hegel the idea of an historical reality becomes visible only subsequently, when the world has already assumed a fixed inner form: "Only one word more concerning the desire to teach the world what it ought to be. For such a purpose, philosophy, at least, always comes too late. Philosophy as the thought of the world does not appear until reality has completed its formative process and made itself ready. History thus corroborates the teachings of the conception that only in the maturity of reality does the ideal appear as the counterpart to the real, apprehends the real world in its substance, and shapes it into an intellectual kingdom. When philosophy paints its grey in grey, one form of life has become old, and by means of grey it cannot be rejuvenated, but only known. The owl of Minerva takes its flight only when the shades of night are gathering." In the conservative mentality, the "owl of Minerva" does indeed begin its flight only with the approaching twilight.

In its original form, conservative mentality was . . . not concerned with ideas. It was its liberal opponent who, so to speak, forced it into this arena of conflict. The peculiar characteristic of intellectual development seems to lie precisely in the fact that the most recent antagonist dictates the tempo and the form of the battle. Certainly there is little truth in the so-called progressive idea that only the new has the prospect for further existence, and that all else dies off gradually. Rather, the older, driven by the newer, must continuously transform itself and must accommodate itself to the level of the most recent opponent. Thus, at present, those who have been operating with earlier modes of thought, when confronted with sociological arguments must also have recourse to these same methods. In the same manner, at the beginning of the nineteenth century, the liberal-intellectualist mode of thought compelled the conservatives to interpret themselves by intellectualist means.

It is interesting to observe that the original conservative social classes, which earlier had acquired stability through closeness to the land did not succeed in the theoretical interpretation of their own position, and that the discovery of the conservative idea became the work of a body of ideologists who attached themselves to the conservatives.

The accomplishment in this direction of the conservative romantics, and particularly Hegel, consisted in their intellectual analysis of the meaning of conservative existence. With this as a point of departure, they provided an intellectual interpretation of an attitude towards the world which was already implicit in actual conduct but which had not yet become explicit. Hence, in the case of the conservatives, what corresponds to the *idea* is in substance something quite different from the liberal idea. It was Hegel's great achievement to set up against the liberal idea a conservative counterpart, not in the sense of artificially concocting an attitude and a mode of behaviour, but rather by raising an already present mode of experience to an intellectual level and by emphasizing the distinctive characteristics that mark it off from the liberal attitude towards the world.

The conservatives looked upon the liberal idea which characterized the period of the Enlightenment as something vaporous and lacking in concreteness. And it was from this angle that they levelled their attack against it and depreciated it. Hegel saw in it nothing more than a mere "opinion"—a bare image—a pure possibility behind which one takes refuge, saves oneself, and escapes from the demands of the hour.

As opposed to this mere "opinion," this bare subjective image, the conservatives conceived of the idea as rooted in and expressing itself concretely in the living reality of the here and now. Meaning and reality, norm and existence, are not separate here, because the utopian, the "concretized idea," is in a vital sense present in this world. What in liberalism is merely a formal norm, in conservatism acquires concrete content in the prevailing laws of the state. In the objectifications of culture, in art and in science, spirituality unfolds itself, and the idea expresses itself in tangible fullness. . . .

Although it is true that the utopia, or the idea, has become completely congruous with concretely existing reality, i.e. has been assimilated into it, this mode of experience—at least at the highest point in the creative period of this current—nevertheless does not lead to an elimination of tensions and to an inert and passive acceptance of the situation as it is. A certain amount of tension between idea and existence arises from the fact that not every element of this existence embodies meaning, and that it is always necessary to distinguish between what is essential and what is nonessential, and that the present continually confronts us with new tasks and problems which have not yet been mastered. In order to arrive at some norm for orientation, we should not depend on subjective impulses, but must call upon those forces and ideas which have become objectified in us and in our past, upon the spirit which, up to now, has operated through us to create these, our works. But this idea, this spirit, has not been rationally conjured up and has not been arbitrarily chosen as the best among a number of possibilities. It is either in us, as a "silently working force" (Savigny), subjectively perceived, or as an entelechy which has unfolded itself in the collective creations of the community, of the folk, the nation, or the state as an inner form which, for the most part, is perceivable morphologically. . . . In all the varieties of these quests for the "inner form" the same conservative attitude of determinateness persists and, when projected outward, finds expression also in the emphasis on historical determinateness. According to this view and from the standpoint of this attitude towards the world man is by no means absolutely free. Not all things in general and each thing in particular are possible at every moment and in every historical community. The inner form of historical individuality existing at any given time, be it that of an individual personality or of a folk spirit, and the external conditions together with the past that lies behind it, determine the shape of things that are to be. It is for this reason that the historical configuration existing at any given time cannot be artificially constructed, but grows like a plant from its seed.

Even the conservative form of the utopia, the notion of an idea embedded and expressed in reality, is in the last analysis intelligible only in the light of its struggles with the other coexistent forms of utopia. Its immediate antagonist is the liberal idea which has been translated into rationalistic terms. Whereas in the latter, the normative, the "should" is accentuated in experience, in conservatism the emphasis shifts to existing reality, the "is." The fact of the mere existence of a thing endows it with a higher value, be it, as in the case of Hegel, with the tendencies which cluster around the opposite poles that essentially determine modern thought. In the struggle with its bourgeois opponent, Marxism discovered anew that in historical and political matters there can be no "pure theory." It sees that behind every theory there lie collective points of view. The phenomenon of collective thinking, which proceeds according to interests and social and existential situations, Marx spoke of as ideology.

In this case, as so often in political struggles, an important discovery was made, which, once it became known, had to be followed up to its final conclusion. This was the more so since this discovery contained the heart of the problem of political thought in general. The concept ideology serves to point out the problem, but the problem is thereby by no means solved or cleared up. A thoroughgoing clarification is attainable only by getting rid of the one-sidedness inherent in the original conception. First of all, therefore, it will be necessary for our purpose to make two corrections. To begin with, it could easily be shown that those who think in socialist and communist terms discern the ideological element only in the thinking of their opponents while regarding their own thought as entirely free from any taint of ideology. As sociologists there is no reason why we should not apply to Marxism the perceptions which it itself has produced, and point out from case to case its ideological character. Moreover, it should be explained that the concept "ideology" is being used here not as a negative value-judgment, in the sense of insinuating a conscious political lie, but is intended to designate the outlook inevitably associated with a given historical and social situation, and the *Weltanschauung* and style of thought bound up with it. This meaning of the term, which bears more closely on the history of thought, must be sharply differentiated from the other meaning. Of course, we do not deny that in other connections it may also serve to reveal conscious political lies.

Through this procedure nothing that has a positive value for scientific research in the notion of ideology has been discarded. The great revelation it affords is that every form of historical and political thought is essentially conditioned by the life situation of the thinker and his groups. It is our task to disentangle this insight from its one-sided political encrustation, and to elaborate in a systematic manner the thesis that how one looks at history and how one construes a total situation from given facts, depends on the position one occupies within society. In every historical and political contribution it is possible to because of the higher rationality embodied in it, or, as in the case Stahl, because of the mystifying and fascinating effects of its ve irrationality. . . .

The time-sense of this mode of experience and thought is complete opposed to that of liberalism. Whereas for liberalism the future wa everything and the past nothing, the conservative mode of experiencin time found the best corroboration of its sense of determinateness in discovering the significance of the past, in the discovery of time as the creator of value. Duration . . . existed for liberalism only in so far as henceforth it gives birth to progress. But for conservatism everything that exists has a positive and nominal value merely because it has come into existence slowly and gradually. Consequently not only is attention turned to the past and the attempt made to rescue it from oblivion, but the presentness and immediacy of the whole past becomes an actual experience. In this view, history can no longer be thought of as a mere unilinear extension of time, nor does it consist in merely joining on to the line which leads from the present to the future that which led from the past to the present. The conception of time here in question has an imaginary third dimension which it derives from the fact that the past is experienced as virtually present. "The life of the contemporary spirit is a cycle of stages, which on the one hand still have a synchronous coexistence, and only from another view appear as a sequence in time that has passed. The experiences which the spirit seems to have behind it, exist also in the depths of its present being." (Hegel.)

MARXISM: THE LAST IDEOLOGY *

Karl Mannheim

In our treatment of socialist theory we are not for the time being differentiating between socialism and communism, for we are here concerned not so much with the plethora of historical phenomena as

---

* Reprinted by permission of Routledge & Kegan Paul, Ltd., from Karl Mannheim, *Ideology and Utopia*, London: Kegan Paul, Trench, Trubner & Co., Ltd., 1936, pp. 110–119.

determine from what vantage point the objects were observed. However, the fact that our thinking is determined by our social position is not necessarily a source of error. On the contrary, it is often the path to political insight. The significant element in the conception of ideology, in our opinion, is the discovery that political thought is integrally bound up with social life. This is the essential meaning of the oft-quoted sentence, "It is not the consciousness of men that determines their existence but, on the contrary, their social existence which determines their consciousness." [1]

But closely related to this is another important feature of Marxist thought, namely a new conception of the relationship between theory and practice. Whereas the bourgeois theorist devoted a special chapter to setting forth his ends, and whereas this always proceeded from a normative conception of society, one of the most significant steps Marx took was to attack the utopian element in socialism. From the beginning he refused to lay down an exhaustive set of objectives. There is no norm to be achieved that is detachable from the process itself: "Communism for us is not a condition that is to be established nor an ideal to which reality must adjust itself. We call communism the actual movement which abolishes present conditions. The conditions under which this movement proceeds result from those now existing."

If to-day we ask a communist, with a Leninist training, what the future society will actually be like, he will answer that the question is an undialectical one, since the future itself will be decided in the practical dialectical process of becoming. But what is this practical dialectical process?

It signifies that we cannot calculate *a priori* what a thing should be like and what it will be like. We can influence only the general trend of the process of becoming. The everpresent concrete problem for us can only be the next step ahead. It is not the task of political thought to set up an absolute scheme of what should be. Theory, even including communist theory, is a function of the process of becoming. The dialectical relationship between theory and practice consists in the fact that, first of all, theory arising out of a definitely social impulse clarifies the situation. And in the process of clarification reality undergoes a change. We thereby enter a new situation out of which a new theory emerges. The process is, then, as follows: (1) Theory is a function of

[1] Karl Marx, *A Contribution to the Critique of Political Economy*, tr. by N. I. Stone (Chicago, 1913), pp. 11–12.

reality; (2) This theory leads to a certain kind of action; (3) Action changes the reality, or in case of failure, forces us to a revision of the previous theory. The change in the actual situation brought about by the act gives rise to a new theory.[2]

This view of the relationship between theory and practice bears the imprint of an advanced stage in the discussion of the problem. One notes that it was preceded by the onesidedness of an extreme intellectualism and a complete irrationalism, and that it had to circumvent all the dangers which were already revealed in bourgeois and conservative thought and experience. The advantages of this solution lie in the fact that it has assimilated the previous formulation of the problem, and in its awareness of the fact that in the realm of politics the usual run of thought is unable to accomplish anything. On the other hand, this outlook is too thoroughly motivated by the desire for knowledge to fall into a complete irrationalism like conservatism. The result of the conflict between the two currents of thought is a very flexible conception of theory. A basic lesson derived from political experience which was most impressively formulated by Napoleon in the maxim, *"On s'engage, puis on voit,"* [3] here finds its methodological sanction.[4] Indeed, political thought cannot be carried on by speculating about it from the outside. Rather thought becomes illuminated when a concrete

[2] "When the proletariat by means of the class struggle changes its position in society and thereby the whole social structure, in taking cognizance of the changed social situation, i.e. of itself, it finds itself face to face not merely with a new object of understanding, but also changes its position as a knowing subject. The theory serves to bring the proletariat to a consciousness of its social position, i.e. it enables it to envisage itself—simultaneously both as an object and a subject in the social process." (Georg Lukács, *Geschichte und Klassenbewusstsein,* Berlin, 1923.)

"This consciousness in turn becomes the motive force of new activity, since theory becomes a material force once it seizes the masses." (Marx-Engels, *Nachlass,* i, p. 392.)

[3] Indeed both Lenin and Lukács, as representatives of the dialectical approach, find justification in this Napoleonic maxim.

[4] "Revolutionary theory is the generalization of the experiences of the labour movement in all countries. It naturally loses its very essence if it is not connected with revolutionary practice, just as practice gropes in the dark if its path is not illumined by revolutionary theory. But theory can become the greatest force in the labour movement if it is indissolubly bound up with revolutionary practice, for it alone can give to the movement confidence, guidance, strength, and understanding of the inner relations between events and it alone can help practice to clarify the process and direction of class movements in the present and near future." (Joseph Stalin, *Foundations of Leninism,* rev. ed., New York and London, 1932, pp. 26–7.)

situation is penetrated, not merely through acting and doing, but also through the thinking which must go with them.

Socialist-communist theory is then a synthesis of intuitionism and a determined desire to comprehend phenomena in an extremely rational way. Intuitionism is present in this theory because it denies the possibility of exact calculations of events in advance of their happening. The rationalist tendency enters because it aims to fit into a rational scheme whatever novelty comes to view at any moment. At no time is it permissible to act without theory, but the theory that arises in the course of action will be on a different level from the theory that went before.[5] It is especially revolutions that create a more valuable type of knowledge. This constitutes the synthesis which men are likely to make when they live in the midst of irrationality and recognize it as such, but do not despair of the attempt to interpret it rationally. Marxist thought is akin to conservative thought in that it does not deny the existence of an irrational sphere and does not try to conceal it as the bureaucratic mentality does, or treat it in a purely intellectual fashion as if it were rational, as liberal-democratic thinkers do. It is distinguished from conservative thought, however, in that it conceives of this relative irrationality as potentially comprehensible through new methods of rationalization. For even in this type of thought, the sphere of the irrational is not entirely irrational, arbitrary, or incomprehensible. It is true that there are no statically fixed and definite laws to which this creative process conforms, nor are there any exactly recurring sequences of events, but at the same time only a limited number of situations can occur even here. And this after all is the decisive consideration. Even when new elements in historical development emerge they do not constitute merely a chain of unexpected events; the political

[5] Revolution, particularly, creates the situation propitious to significant knowledge: "History in general, the history of revolutions in particular, has always been richer, more varied, and variform, more vital and 'cunning' than is conceived of by the best parties, by the most conscious vanguards of the most advanced classes. This is natural, for the best vanguards express the consciousness, will, passions, and fancies of but tens of thousands, whereas the revolution is effected at the moment of the exceptional exaltation and exertion of all the human faculties—consciousness, will, passion, phantasy, of tens of millions, spurred on by the bitterest class war." (N. Lenin, *"Left" Communism: an Infantile Disorder*, published by the Toiler, n.d. pp. 76–7, also New York and London, 1934.)

It is interesting to observe that from this point of view revolution appears not as an intensification of the passions resident in men nor as mere irrationality. This passion is valuable only because it makes possible the fusion of the accumulated rationality tested out experimentally in the individual experiences of millions.

sphere itself is permeated by tendencies which, even though they are subject to change, through their very presence do nevertheless determine to a large extent the various possibilities.

Therefore, the first task of Marxism is the analysis and rationalization of all those tendencies which influence the character of the situation. Marxist theory has elaborated these structural tendencies in a threefold direction. First, it points out that the political sphere in a given society is based on and is always characterized by the state of productive relations prevailing at the time.[6] The productive relations are not regarded statically as a continually recurring economic cycle, but, dynamically, as a structural interrelationship which is itself constantly changing through time.

Secondly, it sees that changes in this economic factor are most closely connected with transformations in class relations, which involves at the same time a shift in the kinds of power and an ever-varying distribution of power.

But, thirdly, it recognizes that it is possible to understand the inner structure of the system of ideas dominating men at any period and to determine theoretically the direction of any change or modification in this structure.

Still more important is the fact that these three structural patterns are not considered independently of one another. It is precisely their reciprocal relations which are made to constitute a single group of problems. The ideological structure does not change independently of the class structure, and the class structure does not change independently of the economic structure. And it is precisely the interconnection and intertwining of this threefold formulation of the problem, the economic, the social, and the ideological, that gives to Marxist ideas their singularly penetrating quality. Only this synthetic power enables it to formulate ever anew the problem of the structural totality of society, not only for the past but also for the future. The paradox lies in the fact that Marxism recognizes relative irrationality and never loses sight of it. But unlike the historical school it does not content itself with a mere acceptance of the irrational. Instead it tries to eliminate as much of it as possible by a new effort at rationalization.

[6] "The mode of production in material life determines the general character of the social, political, and spiritual processes of life." (Marx, *Contribution to the Critique of Political Economy*, tr. by N. I. Stone, Chicago, 1913, p. 11.)

Here again the sociologist is confronted with the question of the general historical-social form of existence and the particular situation from which the mode of thought peculiar to Marxism arose. How can we explain its singular character which consists in combining an extreme irrationalism with an extreme rationalism in such a manner that out of this fusion there arises a new kind of "dialectical" rationality?

Considered sociologically, this is the theory of an ascendant class which is not concerned with momentary successes, and which therefore will not resort to a "putsch" as a means for seizing power, but which, because of its inherent revolutionary tendencies, must always be sensitive and alert to unpredictable constellations in the situation. Every theory which arises out of a class position and is based not on unstable masses but on organized historical groups must of necessity have a long-range view. Consequently, it requires a thoroughly rationalized view of history on the basis of which it will be possible at any moment to ask ourselves where we are now and at what stage of development does our movement find itself.[7]

Groups of pre-capitalistic origin, in which the communal element prevails, may be held together by traditions or by common sentiments alone. In such a group, theoretical reflection is of entirely secondary importance. On the other hand, in groups which are not welded together primarily by such organic bonds of community life, but which merely occupy similar positions in the social-economic system, rigorous theorizing is a prerequisite of cohesion. Viewed sociologically this extreme need for theory is the expression of a class society in which persons must be held together not by local proximity but by similar circumstances of life in an extensive social sphere. Sentimental ties are effective only within a limited spatial area, while a theoretical *Weltanschauung* has a unifying power over great distances. Hence a rationalized conception of history serves as a socially unifying factor for groups dispersed in space, and at the same time furnishes continuity to generations which continuously grow up into similar social conditions. In the formation of classes, a similar position in the social order and a unifying theory are of primary importance. Emotional ties which subsequently spring up are only a reflection of the already existing

[7] "Without a revolutionary theory there can be no revolutionary movement." (Lenin, *What Is To Be Done?* New York and London, 1931.)

situation and are always more or less regulated by theory. Despite this extreme rationalizing tendency, which is implicit in the proletarian class position, the limits of the rationality of this class are defined by its oppositional and, particularly, by its allotted revolutionary position.

Revolutionary purpose prevents rationality from becoming absolute. Even though in modern times the tendency toward rationalization proceeds on such an extensive scale that revolts, which originally were only irrational outbursts, are organized on this plane after a bureaucratic fashion, still there must remain somewhere in our conception of history and our scheme of life a place for the essential irrationality which goes with revolution.

Revolution means that somewhere there is an anticipation of and an intent to provoke a breach in the rationalized structure of society. It necessitates, therefore, a watchfulness for the favourable moment in which the attack must be risked. If the whole social and political sphere were conceived of as thoroughly rationalized, it would imply that we would no longer have to be on the lookout for such a breach. The moment, however, is nothing more than that irrational element in the "here and now," which every theory, by virtue of its generalizing tendency, obscures. But since, so long as one needs and wants revolution, one cannot allow this favourable moment, during which the breach occurs, to pass, there develops a gap in the theoretical picture which indicates that the irrational element is valued for what it really is—is valued essentially in its irrationality.

All this dialectical thinking begins by rationalizing what seemed to the historical-conservative groups totally irrational; it does not, however, go so far in its rationalizing tendency as to yield a totally static picture of what is in process of becoming.

This element of the irrational is embodied in the concept of dialectical transformation. The dominant tendencies in the political sphere are not here construed as mathematically calculable combinations of forces, but rather as capable, at a certain point, of sudden transformation when thrown out of the orbit of their original tendencies. Naturally, this transformation is never subject to prediction; on the contrary, it always depends on the revolutionary act of the proletariat. Thus intellectualism is by no means deemed legitimate in all situations. Quite on the contrary, there appear to be two occasions in which the intuition necessary to comprehend the situation is aroused. First, it always remains incalculable and is left for political intuition to ascertain when the situation is ripe for revolutionary transformation and, second, historical events are never so exactly determinable in advance that it is superfluous to invoke action to change them.

Marxist thought appears as the attempt to rationalize the irrational. The correctness of this analysis is vouched for by the fact that to the extent that Marxian proletarian groups rise to power, they shake off the dialectical elements of their theory and begin to think in the generalizing methods of liberalism and democracy, which seek to arrive at universal laws, whilst those who, because of their position, still have to resort to revolution, cling to the dialectical element (Leninism).

Dialectical thinking is in fact rationalistic but it culminates in irrationalism. It is constantly striving to answer two questions:—first, what is our position in the social process at the moment? second, what is the demand of the moment? Action is never guided simply by impulse but by a sociological understanding of history. Nevertheless it is not to be assumed that irrational impulses can be entirely eliminated by a logical analysis of the situation and of momentary occurrences. Only through acting in the situation do we address questions to it, and the answer we derive is always in the form of the success or failure of the action. Theory is not torn from its essential connection with action, and action is the clarifying medium in which all theory is tested and develops.

The positive contribution of this theory is that out of its own concrete social experience it shows more and more convincingly that political thought is essentially different from other forms of theorizing. This dialectical mode of thought is further significant in that it has incorporated within itself the problems of both bourgeois rationalism and the irrationalism of historicism.

THE SOCIOLOGY OF THE INTELLECTUAL *

Joseph A. Schumpeter

Joseph A. Schumpeter (1883–1950) was an Austrian economist of great distinction. After teaching at several Austrian and German universities and acting as Austrian Minister of Finance from 1919 to 1920 he came to America where he was a professor of economics at Harvard from 1932 on. Besides some very significant works on business cycles and economic development, he wrote on social classes and imperialism.

. . . Neither the opportunity of attack nor real or fancied grievances are in themselves sufficient to produce, however strongly they may favor, the emergence of active hostility against a social order. For such an atmosphere to develop it is necessary that there be groups to whose interest it is to work up and organize resentment, to nurse it, to voice it and to lead it. The mass of people never develops definite opinions on its own initiative. Still less is it able to articulate them and to turn them into consistent attitudes and actions. All it can do is to follow or refuse to follow such group leadership as may offer itself. Until we have discovered social groups that will qualify for that role our theory of the atmosphere of hostility to capitalism is incomplete.

Broadly speaking, conditions favorable to general hostility to a social system or specific attack upon it will in any case tend to call forth groups that will exploit them. But in the case of capitalist society there is a further fact to be noted: unlike any other type of society, capitalism inevitably and by virtue of the very logic of its civilization creates, educates and subsidizes a vested interest in social unrest.[1]

---

* Reprinted from pp. 145–149, 150–154, *Capitalism, Socialism and Democracy,* Third Edition, by Joseph A. Schumpeter, Copyright 1942, 1947 by Joseph A. Schumpeter; Copyright 1950 by Harper & Brothers. Reprinted with the permission of Harper & Row, Publishers.

[1] Every social system is sensitive to revolt and in every social system stirring up revolt is a business that pays in case of success and hence always attracts both brain and brawn. It did in feudal times—very much so. But warrior nobles who revolted against their superiors attacked individual persons or positions. They did not attack the feudal system as such. And feudal society as a whole displayed no

This type is not easy to define. The difficulty is in fact symptomatic of the character of the species. Intellectuals are not a social class in the sense in which peasants or industrial laborers constitute social classes; they hail from all the corners of the social world, and a great part of their activities consist in fighting each other and in forming the spearheads of class interests not their own. Yet they develop group attitudes and group interests sufficiently strong to make large numbers of them behave in the way that is usually associated with the concept of social classes. Again, they cannot be simply defined as the sum total of all the people who have had a higher education; that would obliterate the most important features of the type. Yet anyone who had—and, save exceptional cases, nobody who had not—is a potential intellectual; and the fact that their minds are all similarly furnished facilitates understanding between them and constitutes a bond. Nor would it serve our purpose to make the concept coextensive with the membership of the liberal professions; physicians or lawyers for instance are not intellectuals in the relevant sense unless they talk or write about subjects outside of their professional competence which no doubt they often do—particularly the lawyers. Yet there is a close connection between the intellectuals and the professions. For *some* professions—especially if we count in journalism—actually do belong almost wholly to the domain of the intellectual type; the members of *all* professions have the opportunity of becoming intellectuals; and many intellectuals take to some profession for a living. Finally, a definition by means of the contrast to manual labor would be much too wide. Yet the Duke of Wellington's "scribbling set" seems to be too narrow. So is the meaning of *hommes de lettres*.

But we might do worse than take our lead from the Iron Duke. Intellectuals are in fact people who wield the power of the spoken and the written word, and one of the touches that distinguish them from other people who do the same is the absence of direct responsibility for practical affairs. This touch in general accounts for another—the absence of that first-hand knowledge of them which only actual experience can give. The critical attitude, arising no less from the intellectual's situation as an onlooker—in most cases also as an outsider—than from the fact that his main chance of asserting himself lies in his

---

tendencies to encourage—intentionally or unintentionally—attacks upon its own social system as a whole.

actual or potential nuisance value, should add a third touch. The profession of the unprofessional? Professional dilettantism? The people who talk about everything because they understand nothing? Bernard Shaw's journalist in *The Doctor's Dilemma*? No, no. I have not said that and I do not mean that. That sort of thing would be still more untrue than it would be offensive. Let us give up trying to define by words and instead define "epideiktically": in the Greek museum we can see the object, nicely labeled. The sophists, philosophers and rhetors—however strongly they objected to being thrown together, they were all of the same genus—of the fifth and fourth centuries B.C. illustrate ideally what I mean. That practically all of them were teachers does not destroy the value of the illustration. . . .

The development of rational thought of course precedes the rise of the capitalist order by thousands of years; all that capitalism did was to give a new impulse and a particular bend to the process. Similarly—leaving aside the Graeco-Roman world—we find intellectuals in thoroughly pre-capitalist conditions, for instance in the Kingdom of the Franks and in the countries into which it dissolved. But they were few in number; they were clergymen, mostly monks; and their written performance was accessible to only an infinitesimal part of the population. No doubt strong individuals were occasionally able to develop unorthodox views and even to convey them to popular audiences. This however in general implied antagonizing a very strictly organized environment—from which at the same time it was difficult to get away—and risking the lot of the heretic. Even so it was hardly possible without the support or connivance of some great lord or chieftain, as the tactics of missionaries suffice to show. On the whole, therefore, intellectuals were well in hand, and kicking over the traces was no joke, even in times of exceptional disorganization and license, such as during the Black Death (in and after 1348).

But if the monastery gave birth to the intellectual of the medieval world, it was capitalism that let him loose and presented him with the printing press. The slow evolution of the lay intellectual was merely an aspect of this process; the coincidence of the emergence of humanism with the emergence of capitalism is very striking. The humanists were primarily philologists but—excellently illustrating a point made above—they quickly expanded into the fields of manners, politics, religion and philosophy. This was not alone due to the contents of the classic works which they interpreted along with their grammar—from the criticism of a text to the criticism of a society, the way is shorter than it seems. Nevertheless, the typical intellectual did not relish the idea of the stake which still awaited the heretic. As a rule, honors and comfort suited him a great deal better. And these were after all to be had only from princes, temporal or spiritual, though the humanists were the first intellectuals to have a public in the modern sense. The critical attitude grew stronger every day. But *social* criticism—beyond what was implied in certain attacks on the Catholic Church and in particular its head—did not flourish under such conditions.

Honors and emoluments can however be had in more than one way. Flattery and subservience are often less remunerative than are their opposites. This discovery was not made by the Aretino but no mortal ever surpassed him in exploiting it. Charles V was a devoted husband but, during his campaigns which kept him from home for many months at a time, he lived the life of a gentleman of his time and class. Very well, the public—and what particularly mattered to Charles, his empress—need never know, provided arguments of the right kind and weight were duly handed to the great critic of politics and morals. Charles paid up. But the point is that this was not simple blackmail which in general benefits one party only and inflicts uncompensated loss on the other. Charles knew why he paid though doubtless it would have been possible to secure silence by cheaper if more drastic methods. He did not display resentment. On the contrary he even went out of his way to honor the man. Obviously he wanted more than silence and, as a matter of fact, he received full value for his gifts.

In a sense, therefore, the Aretino's pen was indeed stronger than the sword. But, perhaps through ignorance, I do not know of comparable instances of that type for the next hundred and fifty years, during which intellectuals do not seem to have played any great role outside and independently of the established professions, mainly the law and the church. Now this setback roughly coincides with the setback in capitalist evolution which in most countries of continental Europe occurred in that troubled period. And the subsequent recovery of capitalist enterprise was similarly shared by the intellectuals. The cheaper book, the cheap newspaper or pamphlet, together with the widening of the public that was in part their product but partly an independent phenomenon due to the access of wealth and weight which came to the industrial bourgeoisie and to the incident increase in the political importance of an anonymous public opinion—all these boons, as well as increasing freedom from restraint, are by-products of the capitalist engine. . . .

How impossible it is to stem the tide within the framework of capitalist society is shown by the failure of the attempts—some of them prolonged and determined—made during that period by practically all European governments to bring the intellectuals to heel. Their histories were nothing but so many different versions of Wilkes' exploits. In capitalist society—or in a society that contains a capitalist element of decisive importance—any attack on the intellectuals must run up against the private fortresses of bourgeois business which, or some of which, will shelter the quarry. Moreover such an attack must proceed according to bourgeois principles of legislative and administrative practice which no doubt may be stretched and bent but will checkmate prosecution beyond a certain point. Lawless violence the bourgeois stratum may accept or even applaud when thoroughly roused or frightened, but only temporarily. In a purely bourgeois regime like that of Louis Philippe, troops may fire on strikers, but the police cannot round up intellectuals or must release them forthwith; otherwise the bourgeois stratum, however strongly disapproving some of their doings, will rally behind them because the freedom it disapproves cannot be crushed without also crushing the freedom it approves.

Observe that I am not crediting the bourgeoisie with an unrealistic dose of generosity or idealism. Nor am I unduly stressing what people think and feel and want—on the importance of which I almost, though not quite, agree with Marx. In defending the intellectuals as a group—not of course every individual—the bourgeoisie defends itself and its scheme of life. Only a government of non-bourgeois nature and non-bourgeois creed—under modern circumstances only a socialist or fascist one—is strong enough to discipline them. In order to do that it would have to change typically bourgeois institutions and drastically reduce the individual freedom of *all* strata of the nation. And such a government is not likely—it would not even be able—to stop short of private enterprise.

From this follows both the unwillingness and the inability of the capitalist order to control its intellectual sector effectively. The unwillingness in question is unwillingness to use methods consistently that are uncongenial to the mentality shaped by the capitalist process; the inability is the inability to do so within the frame of institutions shaped by the capitalist process and without submitting to non-bourgeois rule. Thus, on the one hand, freedom of public discussion involving freedom to nibble at the foundations of capitalist society is inevitable in the long run. On the other hand, the intellectual group cannot help nibbling, because it lives on criticism and its whole position depends on criticism that stings; and criticism of persons and of current events will, in a situation in which nothing is sacrosanct, fatally issue in criticism of classes and institutions.

A few strokes will complete the modern picture. There are the increasing means. There is the increase in the standard of life and in the leisure of the masses that changed and is still changing the composition of the collective patron for the tastes of whom the intellectuals have to provide. There was and is the further cheapening of the book and newspaper and the large-scale newspaper concern. There is now the radio. And there was and is the tendency toward complete removal of restraints, steadily breaking down those short-run attempts at resistance by which bourgeois society proves itself so incompetent and occasionally so childish a disciplinarian.

There is, however, another factor. One of the most important features of the later stages of capitalist civilization is the vigorous expansion of the educational apparatus and particularly of the facilities for higher education. This development was and is no less inevitable than the development of the largest-scale industrial unit,[2] but, unlike the latter, it has been and is being fostered by public opinion and public authority so as to go much further than it would have done under its own steam. Whatever we may think of this from other standpoints and whatever the precise causation, there are several consequences that bear upon the size and attitude of the intellectual group.

First, inasmuch as higher education thus increases the supply of services in professional, quasi-professional and in the end all "white collar" lines beyond the point determined by cost-return considerations,

[2] At present this development is viewed by most people from the standpoint of the ideal of making educational facilities of any type available to all who can be induced to use them. This ideal is so strongly held that any doubts about it are almost universally considered to be nothing short of indecent, a situation not improved by the comments, all too often flippant, of dissentients. Actually, we brush here against a set of extremely complex problems of the sociology of education and educational ideals which we cannot attack within the limits of this sketch. This is why I have confined the above paragraph to two incontestable and noncommittal trivialities that are all we want for the purpose in hand. But of course they do not dispose of the larger problems which must be left aside to testify to the incompleteness of my exposition.

it may create a particularly important case of sectional unemployment.

Second, along with or in place of such unemployment, it creates unsatisfactory conditions of employment—employment in substandard work or at wages below those of the better-paid manual workers.

Third, it may create unemployability of a particularly disconcerting type. The man who has gone through a college or university easily becomes psychically unemployable in manual occupations without necessarily acquiring employability in, say, professional work. His failure to do so may be due either to lack of natural ability—perfectly compatible with passing academic tests—or to inadequate teaching; and both cases will, absolutely and relatively, occur more frequently as ever larger numbers are drafted into higher education and as the required amount of teaching increases irrespective of how many teachers and scholars nature chooses to turn out. The results of neglecting this and of acting on the theory that schools, colleges and universities are just a matter of money, are too obvious to insist upon. Cases in which among a dozen applicants for a job, all formally qualified, there is not one who can fill it satisfactorily, are known to everyone who has anything to do with appointments—to everyone, that is, who is himself qualified to judge.

All those who are unemployed or unsatisfactorily employed or unemployable drift into the vocations in which standards are least definite or in which aptitudes and acquirements of a different order count. They swell the host of intellectuals in the strict sense of the term whose numbers hence increase disproportionately. They enter it in a thoroughly discontented frame of mind. Discontent breeds resentment. And it often rationalizes itself into that social criticism which as we have seen before is in any case the intellectual spectator's typical attitude toward men, classes and institutions especially in a rationalist and utilitarian civilization. Well, here we have numbers; a well-defined group situation of proletarian hue; and a group interest shaping a group attitude that will much more realistically account for hostility to the capitalist order than could the theory—itself a rationalization in the psychological sense—according to which the intellectual's righteous indignation about the wrongs of capitalism simply represents the logical inference from outrageous facts and which is no better than the theory of lovers that their feelings represent nothing but the logical inference from the virtues of the beloved.[3] Moreover our theory also accounts for the fact that this hostility increases, instead of diminishing, with every achievement of capitalist evolution.

Of course, the hostility of the intellectual group—amounting to moral disapproval of the capitalist order—is one thing, and the general hostile atmosphere which surrounds the capitalist engine is another thing. The latter is the really significant phenomenon; and it is not simply the product of the former but flows partly from independent sources, some of which have been mentioned before; so far as it does, it is raw material for the intellectual group to work on. There are give-and-take relations between the two which it would require more space to unravel than I can spare. The general contours of such an analysis are however sufficiently obvious and I think it safe to repeat that the role of the intellectual group consists primarily in stimulating, energizing, verbalizing and organizing this material and only secondarily in adding to it. Some particular aspects will illustrate the principle.

Capitalist evolution produces a labor movement which obviously is not the creation of the intellectual group. But it is not surprising that such an opportunity and the intellectual demiurge should find each other. Labor never craved intellectual leadership but intellectuals invaded labor politics. They had an important contribution to make: they verbalized the movement, supplied theories and slogans for it—class war is an excellent example—made it conscious of itself and in doing so changed its meaning. In solving this task from their own standpoint, they naturally radicalized it, eventually imparting a revolutionary bias to the most bourgeois trade-union practices, a bias most of the non-intellectual leaders at first greatly resented. But there was another reason for this. Listening to the intellectual, the workman is almost invariably conscious of an impassable gulf if not of downright distrust. In order to get hold of him and to compete with non-intellectual leaders, the intellectual is driven to courses entirely unnecessary for the latter who can afford to frown. Having no genuine authority and feeling always in danger of being unceremoniously told to mind his own

[3] The reader will observe that any such theories would be unrealistic even if the facts of capitalism or the virtues of the beloved were actually all that the social critic or the lover believes them to be. It is also important to note that in the overwhelming majority of cases both critics and lovers are obviously sincere: neither psycho-sociological nor psycho-physical mechanisms enter as a rule into the limelight of the Ego, except in the mask of sublimations.

business, he must flatter, promise and incite, nurse left wings and scowling minorities, sponsor doubtful or submarginal cases, appeal to fringe ends, profess himself ready to obey—in short, behave toward the masses as his predecessors behaved first toward their ecclesiastical superiors, later toward princes and other individual patrons, still later toward the collective master of bourgeois complexion. Thus, though intellectuals have not created the labor movement, they have yet worked it up into something that differs substantially from what it would be without them.

The social atmosphere, for the theory of which we have been gathering stones and mortar, explains why public policy grows more and more hostile to capitalist interests, eventually so much so as to refuse on principle to take account of the requirements of the capitalist engine and to become a serious impediment to its functioning. The intellectual group's activities have however a relation to anti-capitalist policies that is more direct than what is implied in their share in verbalizing them. Intellectuals rarely enter professional politics and still more rarely conquer responsible office. But they staff political bureaus, write party pamphlets and speeches, act as secretaries and advisers, make the individual politician's newspaper reputation which, though it is not everything, few men can afford to neglect. In doing these things they to some extent impress their mentality on almost everything that is being done.

The actual influence exerted varies greatly with the state of the political game from mere formulation to making a measure politically possible or impossible. But there is always plenty of scope for it. When we say that individual politicians and parties are exponents of class interests we are at best emphasizing one-half of the truth. The other half, just as important if not more so, comes into view when we consider that politics is a profession which evolves interests of its own—interests that may clash with as well as conform to the interests of the groups that a man or party "represents." Individual and party opinion is, more than anything else, sensitive to those factors in the political situation that directly affect the career or the standing of the individual or party. Some of these are controlled by the intellectual group in much the same sense as is the moral code of an epoch that exalts the cause of some interests and puts the cause of others tacitly out of court.

Finally, that social atmosphere or code of values affects not only policies—the spirit of legislation—but also administrative practice. But again there is also a more direct relation between the intellectual group and bureaucracy. The bureaucracies of Europe are of pre- and extra-capitalist origin. However much they may have changed in composition as the centuries rolled on, they never identified themselves wholly with the bourgeoisie, its interests or its scheme of values, and never saw much more in it than an asset to be managed in the interest of the monarch or of the nation. Except for inhibitions due to professional training and experience, they are therefore open to conversion by the modern intellectual with whom, through a similar education, they have much in common, while the tinge of gentility that in many cases used to raise a barrier has been fading away from the modern civil servant during the last decades. Moreover, in times of rapid expansion of the sphere of public administration, much of the additional personnel required has to be taken directly from the intellectual group—witness this country.

TOTALITARIAN IDEOLOGY *

Carl J. Friedrich and Zbigniew K. Brzezinski

C. J. Friedrich is Eaton Professor of the Science of Government at Harvard. He has written extensively on every aspect of political life and thought, his latest, and most comprehensive work, being Man and His Government *(New York: McGraw-Hill, 1963). Z. K. Brzezinski is professor of public law and government at Columbia University and director of its Research Institute on Communist Affairs. He is the author of many studies of Soviet and East European politics, and especially of the place of ideology in the Soviet system. His most recent book, written with Samuel P. Huntington, is* Political Power: USA/USSR, *(New York: Viking Press, 1963).*

. . . Ideologies are essentially action-related systems of ideas. They typically contain a program and a strategy for its realization and their essential purpose is to unite organizations which are built around them.

* Reprinted by permission of the publishers from C. J. Friedrich and Z. K. Brzezinski, *Totalitarian Dictatorship and Autocracy,* Cambridge, Mass.: Harvard University Press, Copyright, 1956, by the President and Fellows of Harvard College. Pp. 75–78, 80–88.

The rise and development of such ideologies appears to be a feature of the democratic age, . . . and seems to be associated with the development of parties. Parties of reform especially tend to develop such ideologies, which they propose to put into practice upon their assumption of power. In this process, adaptations take place and some of the more utopian aspects of the ideology are eliminated as a concession to reality. Totalitarian parties are an extreme instance of this general trend. By their elimination of all rivals . . . , they monopolize the field and convert their group ideology into a governmental one. But the process of adaptation to "reality" still takes place even though a persistent effort is made to maintain the myth that the ideology is intact, and that the concessions are temporary. Thus Hitler found himself obliged to compromise with big business and indeed to strengthen its position of monopolistic control in the German economy, although his ideology called for "socialism" in the sense of the state protecting the interests of the lower middle classes and the workers. By mobilizing the idea of "leadership" and by making the factory owner or manager the "leader" of the enterprise, he tried to straddle the ideological conflict.

Similarly in the Soviet Union the regime had to face the problem of adjusting the hallowed concept of "withering away of the state" to the new "socialist realities." This concept, highly utopian in its appeal, had been repeatedly stressed in Lenin's writings, in which he quoted Marx and Engels as his authority and emphasized himself that "the proletariat needs only a state which is withering away, i.e., a state so constituted that it begins to wither away immediately, and cannot but wither away."

The abyss between this statement and current Soviet reality is obvious, and the Soviet leaders have not been blind to it. The concept has consequently been redefined to suit the imperatives of power without prima facie invalidating it. Stalin merely stated that

> [the concept] is correct but only on one of two conditions: 1) *if* we study the socialist state only from the angle of internal development of the country, abstracting ourselves in advance from the international factor, isolating, for the convenience of investigation, the country and state from the international situation; or 2) *if* we assume that *socialism* is already victorious in all countries, or in the majority of countries, that a Socialist encirclement exists instead of a *capitalist encirclement,* that there is no more danger of foreign attack, and that there is no more need to strengthen the army and the state.

These illustrations serve to show that an ideology can be more or less "rational" in its elaboration. The Soviet ideology, based as it is upon the allegedly "scientific" findings of Karl Marx and Friedrich Engels, as elaborated by N. Lenin and others, appears to be decidedly more rational than either that of Fascist Italy or Hitler Germany. In the last two instances, the ideology was distinctly "personal," resting, in the case of Mussolini, upon his journalistic writings and more especially his article on fascism in the *Encyclopedia Italiana* (1932); in the case of Hitler, upon *Mein Kampf* written in 1923–24 during his sojourn in jail, and maintained ever after as the gospel of National Socialism. An analysis in terms of antecedent intellectual influences and the like would incline one to differentiate further and call Mussolini's creed more rational than that of Hitler. The degree of "rationality" here involved is that of a rationality of means, rather than ends. For the values in all three ideologies are of a highly emotional sort. This may not make much difference to the skeptic who considers all value judgments beyond rational discourse, but in any case there are differences of degree, and it is certainly permissible to assert that the value judgments at the base of Thomism, Confucianism, and modern constitutionalism are more rational than those of the totalitarian creeds, even if they are not wholly rational.

These totalitarian ideologies can also be classified according to their ultimate values, and this is the more usual and conventional procedure. We then arrive at the very well-known differentiation between the Soviet ideology which is universal in its appeal—"Workers of all the world, unite!"—and the fascist ideologies—which address themselves to a particular people in terms of their grandeur, power, and historical role. In the Soviet ideology, the place of the national group is taken by the proletariat, which is invested with the historical role of liberating mankind from the shackles of industrial capitalism, but Marx and Engels make it very clear that this proletariat, by overthrowing the existing class structure, ultimately eliminates itself and ceases to exist as a proletariat. From this standpoint, social justice appears to be the ultimate value, unless it be the classless society which is its essential condition; for the fascist, this ultimate or highest value is dominion, eventually world dominion, and the strong and pure nation-race is *its* essential condition, as seen by its ideology. Since there are many nations and races, there can theoretically be as many fascisms, and this has actually proven to be the case. Wherever fascism has raised its head, whether in France, England, or the United States, the strength and the purification of the particular nation involved has been in the center of ideological attention. This aspect is an element of weakness in fascist ideologies, as contrasted with the communist ones. The latter have the advantage of an inherent universalism and the consequent ability to cope more readily with the extension of power to other nations (the Soviet Union vis-à-vis Poland, Czechoslovakia, Germany, and so forth, China vis-à-vis Korea, Indochina, and so forth).

It is precisely this doctrinal catholicism which makes communism an effective weapon of combat, not only between nations, but also, and generally unlike fascism, within nations. Fascism, when a spontaneous product of local combustion, by necessity tended to accentuate national distinctiveness and national sovereignty. It emphasized frequently the biological superiority of the given community. Fascism, when imposed on several nations, produced, as it did during World War II, the most vigorous reactions from those nations which it enveloped. Universality based on a restricted nationalist appeal is a contradiction in terms. Actually, Italian Fascism had a good deal of appeal beyond Italy. Similar movements cropped up in Austria, Hungary, Rumania, Spain, France, and Great Britain, and one must not forget that Italian Fascism was, after all, the inspiration for many of Hitler's followers as well as for Hitler himself. Peron also followed the basic line of Italian Fascism. There is a very interesting item in the Italian Fascist catechism used in the youth organizations: "Question: Is Fascism exclusively an Italian phenomenon? Answer: Fascism, as far as its ideas, doctrines and realizations are concerned, is *universal,* because it is in the position of saying to all civilized people *the word of truth without which there cannot be lasting peace in the world; therefore it is the sustainer and creator of a new civilization.*" It should be noted, however, that with this kind of "universalism," while it may be able to arouse imitators, each of the resulting fascist movements will itself seek world, or regional, dominion, and hence be creating obstacles to the extension of effective control by the "creator." Presumably, a fascist France or England would have been at least as vigorous a rival of Italian aspirations to dominion in the Mediterranean as the democratic regimes of these countries were.

Communism, on the other hand, has been markedly successful in operating on the national base for the sake of supranational goals. . . .

In seeking to trace the roots of totalitarian ideology, every kind of link has been argued. Marx and Hegel, Nietzsche and Hobbes, Kant and Rousseau, Plato and Aristotle, St. Augustine, Luther, and Calvin—all have been charged with having forged the ideas that became weapons in the arsenal of the totalitarians. Since the thinkers thus involved are in turn related to many other intellectual trends and views, it is not too much to suggest that the sum of all the arguments is plainly this: totalitarian ideology is rooted in the totality of Western thought and more especially its political thought. To be sure, the key points of emphasis, such as equality, justice, freedom are of so general a nature that they do not lend themselves to very precise analysis in this context. But even more specific points, like the stress on democracy or the state, are similarly elusive. This situation should not surprise anyone, for the programs of action which the totalitarians proclaim are programs cast in terms of the antecedent states of European and American society (with interesting variations introduced in cases such as China) and they must therefore be related to the patterns of ideas associated with these antecedent states. Moreover, since ideology has an instrumental function, . . . totalitarian leaders will fashion their ideological tools to fit the states of mind of the masses they are addressing. For example the idea of progress, so peculiar a product of the Western mind, is embedded in the totalitarian thought so deeply that it would collapse if this idea were eliminated.

It should be clear that this entire discussion of the roots of totalitarian ideology rests upon what answer is given to the question: what is the role of ideas in history? Do ideas have demonstrable effects or are they merely incidental to reality, like the froth on top of the waves of an agitated sea? Many of the writers who have placed major emphasis upon the ideological background of totalitarian movements have failed to realize the full implications of this view. For if ideas are assumed to have significant causal effects upon the course of events, a spiritualistic interpretation of history easily becomes part of the story. A stress upon religious ideas is most especially prone to carry that implication. The common argument that men act in terms of the ideas in their minds does not settle the question of where such ideas come from. If some such notion as inspiration is introduced—Trotsky wrote that revolution is the mad inspiration of history—then one must ask: whose inspiration and by whom inspired? It is evident that many contemporary formulas are merely thinly disguised, feebly secularized ways of saying the same thing that the old Jews had in mind when they claimed that God had given the Tables to Moses. The several totalitarian ideologies are basically trite restatements of certain traditional ideas, arranged in an incoherent way that makes them highly exciting to weak minds.

Their roots are as varied as the backgrounds of the people who expound them and who listen to them. One might illustrate this by the recurrent references in Hitler's *Mein Kampf* to the notion that the end of national glory justifies any means appropriate for its achievement. This "Machiavellism" has been charged to Machiavelli and some of his followers. But what was in Machiavelli, at least for his time, a novel and fairly sophisticated doctrine becomes in Hitler's treatment a crude and banal thought.

In other words, any effort to relate totalitarian ideology more specifically to antecedent thought reveals that the antecedent thought is either distorted to fit the proposition, or completely misrepresented. Thus Hegel is made an exponent of the doctrine that "might makes right," when as a matter of fact, he explicitly and sharply rejected it. Or Hobbes is claimed to believe in the "state regulating everything," when it is quite evident to a casual but unprejudiced reader, that Hobbes was inclined to restrict the sovereign to the police function, that is, to the function of maintaining peace in a given society. If one were to argue all the various statements which have been set forth on this score, one could fill volumes. Such arguments may have a certain value in the market place, where the fighting about these ideas takes place; but on the whole, it is a hopeless enterprise, because the history of ideas is a particularly difficult field of scholarship which is fully mastered by few. In any case, the problem of what an author actually said, and, in the saying of it, what he meant calls for a never-ending search, and the more comprehensive the author, the more divergent the answers. Nonetheless, the discussion of whether the activities of the Soviet Union fit the ideas which Marx and Engles expounded is a source of continuing controversy and debate. A volume such as *The God that Failed* is almost entirely concerned with a discussion of the true meanings of Marxian teachings.

There is no doubt that Marxism owes a great intellectual debt to the traditions, and particularly to the modes of thought, of the French Revolution. The intellectual climate of Europe, of which both Marx and Engels were very much a part, had been fired not only by the slogans, but also by the philosophic content of that great enterprise. As a result, though surely not for the first time in the history of Europe, the intellectual, in his role of interpreter of the past and of the present, reached out to shape the realities of tomorrow. To acknowledge that Marxism is part of that stream is not, however, to establish a causal relationship, for to do so, as some have, is to engage in ex post facto attempts to interpret the ideas and even motivations of eighteenth-century thinkers in terms of categories imposed by the nineteenth- and twentieth-century realities. Nonetheless, it can be shown that the Rousseauistic concept of total democracy can easily degenerate into total dictatorship when the Legislator ceases to be a transient educator and becomes a permanent vanguard acting in behalf of the people. Such concepts as "knowledge" are not far removed from "consciousness," of a class variety, and both need to be instilled in those "who are born free and yet everywhere are in chains." The emphasis on unity, unanimity, and ceaseless participation are suggestive–but no more than that–of the twentieth-century "passion for unanimity" . . . characteristic of the totalitarian systems. And, what is more, it was the French Revolution which gave an outlet to the feeling of rationalistic revolutionaries that society must, and can be, remade in its totality to assure man the liberty which is inherently his. Indeed a dialectical relationship to the religious zealots of the past suggests itself. Like Saint-Just, in the French Revolution, such individuals become the self-appointed guardians of virtue and truth; genuine conflicts of opinion are excluded, and disagreement is condemned as absolutely wrong.

Similarly, the Marxist dialectic contains not only Hegel, but Babeuf and his primitive notions of class struggle. At the same time, Marxian doctrine divorced the utilitarian emphasis on self-interest from the individual, welded it to an economic class, and made it the focal point of the historical movement. Thus various antecedent notions borrowed from different writers and movements were fitted to the requirements of the industrial age and the peasant reaction to the machine. One need not linger, however, on the relationship of Marxism to preceding thought in the western political heritage to prove how complex is the task of establishing meaningful intellectual causation. Within Marxism itself, which developed . . . through schismatic clashes, the problem of elaboration or distortion is continually disputed. For instance, the formation of the new communist regimes in central Europe and Asia, bringing with it the problem of transition from a bourgeois or feudal society to a communist one, has perplexed Soviet ideologues in recent years. For various practical reasons, the theory of the dictatorship of the proletariat, mentioned only once by Marx in his *Critique of the Gotha*

Program and developed by Lenin into something of utmost importance, has become unsuitable for these regions. A completely new terminology and a new interpretation, evolving around the term "People's Democracy" has been developed. The relationship between this terminology and Marx's own view of the postrevolutionary situation is open to dispute.

Disappointed believers in some of the ideas contained in a particular ideology recurrently constitute very strong opponents of the regime based upon such ideology. This is a phenomenon familiar from the history of religion. After all, the story of Christianity is to a considerable extent the story of successive disagreements over what Christ meant, and over the true import of his message. From these disagreements have resulted the successive dissents leading to new sects and churches. Considering the relatively short time that totalitarians have been actively at work, it is surprising how many divergent interpretations have already been expounded and made the basis of schismatic movements.

And yet it is these schisms which provide a real clue to the meaning of the term we have been using–totalitarian ideology. The splits and disagreements on the basic tenets of Marxism, for instance, have served to accentuate the democratic and nondemocratic aspects of that theory. Through a process of political adaptation, differences in degree have become differences in kind, despite the original uniformity of view. Are not then social democracy and communism possibly the products of the same intellectual roots? Do they not claim ancestorship of a common family tree? Are not their basic assumptions to be found essentially in the same body of writings? Despite the necessarily affirmative answers, the distinction between the two schools of thought, when translated into actual practice becomes fundamental and far-reaching–one is totalitarian, the other not.

The translation of an ideology into practice usually serves to reveal certain inadequacies inherent in human foresight. Attempts to picture the future and to prescribe the methods of achieving it clearly cannot conceive of all eventualities, of all possible situations, and communism is further handicapped by the general looseness of its philosophical structure. Consequently the schismatic movements which developed immediately as attempts were made to transform Marxism into political practice were, apart from pure power factors, the inevitable product of such an attempted implementation. When theory is applied to a real-life situation, there are usually only two alternatives: one is to modify theory so as to make it more compatible with the prerequisites of practice, and the other is to attempt to force reality to fit the theory. The totalitarians, by their almost complete rejection of the *status quo,* are inclined to attempt to force history to fit their conception of it. And when such a conception involves a far-reaching idea of the desirable, that is, historically inevitable, scheme of social organization, the efforts to mold society to fit it, and the consequent measures to break down the resistance to it, result in totalitarianism.

Not all the original supporters of such an ideology, however, are willing to go quite so far. This is particularly well demonstrated by the Marxist schism on the issue of evolution *versus* revolution. Marxism embodies both concepts, which are said to be historically inseparable. "Revolution is the midwife of every society," said Marx, but before the midwife sets to work, a lengthy evolutionary process precedes the climatic spasms of the revolution. The inner contradictions of capitalism have to ripen lest the revolution fail by coming too soon. And it is precisely on this time element that conflicting interpretations have clashed. When is the precise moment for revolutionary action?

Bernstein and the so-called Revisionists felt that precipitate revolutionary action would merely intensify the blood flow in the corroded veins of capitalism and thus prolong its life. Key to success, according to Bernstein and the Social Democratic school, was ability to wait, while exacting concessions through participation in the democratic process. Socialism would in time supplant the capitalist order and the revolutionary stage would, in effect, become merely the technical act of taking over. Capitalism would die of old age, and therefore need not be slaughtered. The revolutionary act would consist in burying it, and not in killing it.

The Social Democrats have therefore been unwilling to engage in drastic measures to destroy the capitalist society. Their optimism in the certainty of their success makes them patient and willing to work within the framework of constitutional-capitalist society. Having accepted the perspective of an inevitable historical victory, they are content with the thought that the *status quo* is not going to last.

The totalitarians, however, having announced that the *status quo* is doomed, proceed to prove the correctness of their analysis through measures to effect it. To them, willingness to wait is sheer treason. "Reformism . . . which in effect denies the Socialist revolution and tries to establish socialism peacefully, . . . which preaches not the struggle of classes but their collaboration—this reformism is degenerating from day to day, and is losing all marks of socialism." Lenin and the Bolshevik revolutionaries, accordingly, emphasized that revolutionary action was the key to historical salvation, and that only direct measures aimed at overthrowing the capitalist order would produce its fall. "Great historical questions can be solved only by *violence*," exclaimed Lenin, calling upon the revolutionaries to act as the gravediggers of history and to help repose the remnants of capitalism in the dustbin of antiquity. For, unless a revolutionary party acting as the vanguard of the proletariat acts firmly, the working classes will develop a pacifist trade-union mentality and become the unwitting tools of capitalist measures of self-preservation.

In the Nazi movement, the socially more radical elements were strongly represented in the Storm Troopers, called the Brown Shirts. The SA men were under the command of Captain Roehm, who at the time liked to suggest that all they needed to do was to turn their swastika armbands around to make them red. To be sure, all this argument remained on a very low level, as did the ideological discussion in the Hitler movement generally, but it nonetheless represented a characteristic ideological conflict pointing to the divergent strands in the official creed. There developed also a "leftist" deviation in Italian Fascism which was headed by Giuseppe Bottai, Edmondo Rossoni, and Ugo Spirito. Giovanni Gentile was eventually prevailed upon to make common cause with this group, and his last work, *Genesi e struttura della societa,* expounds the group's general theory. Two reviews, edited by Bottai and Rossoni respectively, expressed these views in a veiled fashion, but it should be noted that these ideas had no support in the inner circles of the party.

In both the Fascist and Nazi movements, actually, the physical presence of the men who formulated the programs prevented the emergence of major splits. The essential postulates of both movements—stressing the leadership principle, the traditional and historical values of the people as contrasted with the "bourgeois" degeneration, the *Etatismo* of Italy and the *Volk* veneration of Nazism, state corporatism but private ownership, the mystic quality of the soil, and last, but not least, the race principle—generally remained unchallenged during their relatively brief existences.

It is noteworthy, however, that both communism and fascism are characterized by their insistence on the revolutionary fulfillment of the "truths" of their doctrines, and it is this insistence that leads to the further conclusions on the necessity of a disciplined party—the elite of the proletariat or of the nation. This party was to eliminate the remnants of the vanquished. Its infallible leadership, through "intuition" or "science," was to effect the conditions which, according to the ideology, are considered necessary for the achievement of its utopian apocalypse. It is precisely this attempt to impose on society a rationally, or rather pseudorationally, conceived pattern of distinctly novel forms of social organization that leads to the totalitarian oppression. And since this oppression is justified in terms of the ideology, this ideology is totalitarian.

The fact that the totalitarian ideology is rooted in the totality of Western ideas raises the question of its relation to democracy and Christianity. On the face of it, these two bodies of thought are the patent antithesis to fascist and communist ideology. The conflict with Christianity was highlighted in the Soviet Union by the Movement of the Godless; in Nazi Germany it led to protracted struggles to establish control over both Protestant and Catholic churches. . . . With regard to democracy, the situation is somewhat more confused since both communists and fascists like to consider themselves true democrats; but, if democracy is defined in constitutional terms as characterized by a genuine competition between two or more parties, a separation of governmental powers, and a judicially enforced protection of individual rights, the conflict is fairly obvious on both the ideological and the practical levels. Yet in spite of these sharp conflicts between totalitarian ideologies on one hand and the Christian and Democratic heritage on the other, it is only within the context of this heritage that the ideologies can be fully understood. Communism is not Christian, but it could not have taken root without the foundations laid by Christian belief in the brotherhood of man and social justice. Perhaps even more important than these substantive links are the habits of mind established by Christianity, and the other religions with a formal theology, such as Buddhism and Mohammedanism, for they establish the cultural habit or trait of relating action programs and norms to elaborate "rational" frameworks. These rational frameworks of theology are then secularized and become ideologies. There is, to put it another way, a style of living involved that calls for transcendent explanations of what is right. When the theological explanations become untenable as a result of the decline of religious faith, these "secular religions" then fill the vacuum. When seen in this perspective, it becomes evident why the totalitarian ideology has become potent even in China, which is not at all a Christian country. The argument is reinforced by the consideration that China inherited, but did not invent, the communist ideology. It seems more than doubtful that Chinese thought would have produced this kind of ideology, and all of Mao's presumed originality in interpreting the Marxist-Leninist heritage provides little more than an attempt at applying it to specific Chinese conditions. It may be well to add that communist ideology has, in a sense, a similar relation to Chinese traditional culture as Christian creeds have had: it is a missionary body of alien thought.

It must be pointed out finally that the relation of the totalitarian ideology to Christian and democratic ideology is a "dialectic" one, that is to say, the relation is antithetical. But, just as antithesis in logic cannot be conceived except in juxtaposition to its thesis, so also in the movement of ideas the root is often the thesis of which the idea or ideology in hand is the antithesis. The importance of this kind of relationship lies not only in the consequent "consanguinity," enabling human beings to shift back and forth between these ideologies, but it also may provide a clue for the next step in the dialectic.

All in all, our discussion has shown that the roots of the totalitarian ideologies, both communist and fascist, are actually intertwined with the entire intellectual heritage of modern man, and that all specific links should be seen, not in terms of causation—of this or that thinker or group of thinkers being "responsible for" the totalitarian ideologies—but as strands of a complex and variegated tapestry. The specific totalitarian ingredient, namely, the employment, even glorification, of violence for the realization of the goals which the ideology posits, is largely absent from the thought of those whose ideas these ideologies have utilized, and, in utilizing them, distorted.